The Pe Strongman's Experience

Real stories and the Lessons Learned While Becoming A Modern
Day Man of Steel

ERIC MOSS

ERIC MOSS

ISBN: 1512114472
ISBN-13: 978-1512114478

FOREWORD
By "The Iron Tamer" David Whitley

Strength comes in many shapes and sizes. So do Strongmen. Over the few short years I have been involved as a professional in the world of strength, I have crossed paths with many people who all share the same common interest - a fascination with the state of superhuman strength. I am fortunate enough to have met many of the legends of this incredible sub-culture, as well as many peers who have the unquenchable desire to find that power within and carry the banner of the old-time strongmen into the future.

I vividly remember my first meeting with Eric Moss. I had been practicing feats for a very short time; Eric was a young fitness professional fascinated by strength and full of questions after seeing some of my feats (fueled by beer) at an impromptu exhibition in a hotel lobby. Our bond began with our common interests in strength and Heavy Metal music. It has only gotten stronger since then.

I was there when he met his first strongman mentor, the late Greg Matonick. I had the gut-wrenching experience of being the guy who told Eric of Greg's passing as well.

I have watched him grow from an enthusiast to a novice to a legitimate steel-bending, license-plate-destroying strongman. The story he tells in this book shows his true love of the art. It shows his respect for all who came before him and his passion for helping everyone he comes in contact with to become a little bit better. I am honored to call him my friend and to share this path with him.

Iron Tamer Dave Whitley
Feb 2015

ERIC MOSS

CONTENTS

DEDICATION

This book is dedicated to the memory of my first mentor New Jersey's Superman, Greg Matonick. You changed everything for me and I know that you are watching my performances from the best seat in the house. None of this would have been possible without you as my guide, my mentor and my friend. I will keep your name alive with this book, with every steel bar that I bend and with every belief that is changed when somebody witnesses the power that you showed me I had. The power we all have.

A very special nod goes out to Hairculese Chris Rider for contributing his expertise, Slim the Hammer Man and the Mighty Atom for inspiring all of us and to the Iron Tamer David Whitley for introducing me to this journey, my mentors and many of the people who would go on to inspire me.

BEHOLD ...

YOU ARE ABOUT TO ENTER A
DOORWAY WHERE DREAMS
BECOME REALITY, AND

WHAT SEEMS

SUPERHUMAN

WILL BECOME NORMAL.

PLEASE LEAVE ALL DOUBT,
FEAR AND NEGATIVITY
OUTSIDE, AND BRING IN ONLY
YOUR DESIRE AND FAITH .....

Photo credit Kira Matonick

MY STORY STARTING FROM THE BEGINNING

I suppose I got my first lesson in perseverance from my parents.

When I was a baby I was born with a lot of potential. Dad graduated from Penn State University with a degree in physics. Mom graduated at the top of her class from a nursing school in the Philippines. Both of them loved me from the day I was born and as I understand it (I was too young to remember) my mom even denied the drugs they offered her for the pain when it came time to deliver me into the world.

My parents would do anything and everything they could to try and help me, but unfortunately not everything was in their control. I was born allergic to just about everything on God's green Earth. It would express itself as severe eczema putting a rash on the crooks of my elbows and behind my knees whenever I ate something I was allergic to, which was a lot. I was allergic to her milk, I was allergic to baby formula, goat's milk, soy milk and just about anything you can think of would keep me up all night trying to tear my skin off with my fingernails.

In fact, one of my earliest memories was having an allergy test done and reacting harshly to it. I was very close to going to the emergency room because of it.. The constant discomfort would keep me awake making it difficult to get quality sleep.

With needing to feed their baby, it wasn't like mom and dad could just give up...they HAD to find something that I could eat. Parents' love for their child is a very strong force that has a lot of tenacity behind it. They kept searching and searching and eventually found something I could digest. It ended up being some kind of weird baby formula that was made from the

1

hearts of cattle (sounds metal doesn't it? \m/). It was difficult to get the right kind of nutrition a developing child needs with all of these crazy restrictions, but my parents did the best job that could have been done. They didn't pull punches when it came to my wellbeing.

With eczema constantly attacking, I would develop extreme rashes on the insides of my elbows, behind my knees and on my neck. If you look at the skin on my elbows closely, you'll notice it isn't regular skin. It is scar tissue because of the constant scratching without it ever getting a chance to heal properly.

When it itched, I couldn't dig deep enough. When it didn't itch, it was very painful. There were plenty of times when I couldn't straighten out an arm or leg for fear of ripping my skin open. I had to limp around on more than one occasion because of this and it would make me feel like an outsider because none of the other children had this going on.

When the other children would ask me about it, even though looking back it was a child's curiosity, I always felt like they were repulsed by it. It made it hard to feel accepted when all the other kids were eating one thing and I was eating my own special thing that wasn't quite as good.

As I got a tad bit older in grade school, I had a hard time focusing on school. Try as I might, I just couldn't settle my mind on what the teacher wanted me to focus on. Often times people would mistake what I had with something else.

A teacher actually told me "You are a lazy little boy and will never amount to anything." That is not something anybody should EVER tell a child. It turns out what this misinformed teacher mistook for laziness was actually attention deficit disorder and the real kind too. I actually am a hard worker when I'm focused, but I wasn't able to focus on school as much as I tried and yes, I really did try.

Was the attention deficit disorder caused by difficulty getting proper nutrition? To be honest, I'm not sure. But I do know it was very difficult to focus on school when there were so many distractions, even if the distractions were stupid things like a dot on my desk or a spot on the floor.

Having the diagnosis of attention deficit disorder I was prescribed a drug called Ritalin. Yes, Ritalin helped me concentrate on my schoolwork but it wasn't without its own consequences. For one thing, it caused me to be extremely shy and unable/unwilling to stand up for myself, which made me an easy target for bullies until they eventually got bored because I was too pathetic to be worth their time.

Just ignoring them may have been effective at making them stop harassing me but it's not the best thing for developing confidence. Being extremely shy and withdrawn made it very difficult to make friends in school since conversations would be only one way. It felt as if my lips were glued shut. Girls wanted nothing to do with me either. Why would they want to date a loser like me?

In addition to the personality suppressant effects I experienced, Ritalin also was an appetite suppressant. I never had the heart to tell my mom this but I threw away most of my school lunches because one bite made me want to gag. There was nothing wrong with the way they tasted; it was just what the drugs side effects were. Anybody who knows me now, knows I have a healthy appetite.

Being shy and withdrawn by day because of the Ritalin, I had a tendency to bottle up everything I was feeling. When it would wear off, I don't know if it was because I was becoming a teenager and the hormones were kicking in or what, but I would be a bit of a loose cannon when it wore off. Let this be my official public apology for being a jerk. I'm sorry. I simply wasn't myself.

With everything I experienced with it, I'll never understand why anyone would want to voluntarily abuse that stuff.

THE TURNING POINT

In high school, enough was enough, and I made the decision that I would never take it again. Looking back, I think my experiences with Ritalin are why I never got involved with drugs. Instead I turned to martial arts, starting with Tae Kwon Do then moving on to Isshinryu Karate and Judo. I also started training with calisthenics and weight training to help improve my martial arts. With those things going, it not only helped me gain the focus that I would need to help with school work (though I'll admit in high-school I wasn't really into my school work), but what was more important was that it also gave me the self-confidence and positive self-image I needed to allow my true personality to finally be revealed. In doing so I found a passion for strength and fitness.

Using that passion for strength and fitness, I decided to become a personal trainer part-time. With that goal and knowing people were going to be paying me good money, I had the mindset that I needed to know stuff they didn't and this gave me desire to learn everything I could about strength and fitness. Through reading, I uncovered hints about the history of old-time *strongmanism*.

The very first place I had ever seen anything about the history of *strongmanism* was in the Bodybuilding Encyclopedia written by Arnold Schwarzenegger. It wasn't much to be honest, a three-page spread, and it didn't leave a great impression on me. It was mainly a nod to physical culture, which was a big part of *strongmanism* (the old physical culturists were strong after all and enjoyed exhibiting their strength). Bodybuilding competitions developed as a natural progression from the aesthetics of physical culture.

Another place I had seen elements of *strongmanism* was one day when I was

5

watching professional wrestling on TV and saw Mark Henry roll up a frying pan with his bare hands. Mark Henry was a very big and an extremely strong man and he looked the part too. It was a publicity stunt meant to promote him as a professional wrestler, but it was the very first feat of that nature I had ever seen and needless to say I was very impressed. Impressed, but Mark Henry is a big strong guy. I'm maybe half his size.

One day as I was out Christmas shopping in a local bookstore I came upon a book called *Enter the Kettlebell*, written by Pavel Tsatsouline. In it he talked about the strongmen of old ripping open horseshoes and I thought to myself "Good lord, ripping open a horseshoe?!?! That's incredibly strong!" I imagined what it must be like to be able to do that.

Another day I was at a seminar learning how to get more clients for my personal training business, I bumped into another personal trainer who was an up and coming strongman. His name was "The Iron Tamer" David Whitley and we hit it off right off the bat.

Dave is a big bear of a man from Nashville. Not incredibly tall, but his forearms are massive and he is a thick guy packed with power. I had seen footage of Dave making kettlebells dance while airborne and picking people up over his head on YouTube and knew he was a senior instructor for a training certification called RKC (Russian Kettlebell Challenge). RKC, at the time (2008), was the go to source for people looking to get stronger with kettlebells and was led by Pavel Tsatsouline, the guy who wrote *Enter the Kettlebell*, where I first became enamored with old-time *strongmanism*. It was also the training system I had used on myself.

Sometime during the seminar someone came in with a set of frying pans and handed it to him. The three frying pans were different in size, a small, a medium and a large (I believe it was six, eight and twelve inches respectively). He grabbed the small one, rolled it up with his bare hands and broke the handle off. Then he took the medium-size frying pan and rolled it around the small one and broke the handle off. Then he took the third frying pan and rolled it around the first two. Three frying pans rolled into one.

This marked the very first old-time feat of strength performed by an old-time performing strongman that I had ever witnessed live. It left an impression on me. Later I would realize what an important impression it would make.

We kept in touch and one day, as I was internet stalking Dave, I found a link to Dennis Rogers' website and promotional video. In this video Dennis Rogers, held back Air Force T-34s and Harley Davidsons taking off at full throttle, bent wrenches and rolled up frying pans.

What?!

This is real?!

People really can do this stuff?!

Not only that, but Dennis didn't appear to be a large man like Mark Henry. This was incredible to me because up until that point everything I had seen had been isolated feats. That was when I saw people who really do this crazy stuff and the seeds for a dream had been planted in my mind.

Fast forward a short time and there was another seminar teaching personal trainers how to grow their businesses again, this time it's only about a half hour from where I was living. Dave tells me he is going to be up and asks if I would assist him in putting some of the other personal trainers there through a workout he named "the furnace" for its ability to raise the temperature of a room.

It's hard to explain, but I felt like we were separate from the other trainers there. Maybe it's because they seemed to all be looking for stuff to try to market their clients while we were trying to find creative ways to highlight the importance of strength in a training program. I don't know exactly what it was. Maybe it was because we all felt like we were just different, not that the others there were less than us, just different. It's difficult to explain really.

"We're going to grab a bite to eat, you want to come with?" Dave asked me.

"I'd love to."

"Cool, we're going to head up to the room first, come on up."

We walk through the door of his hotel room. Dave shared the room with another instructor named BJ and as we were all talking about the events of the day Dave pulled out a pair of wraps and a couple nails and starts bending them. Then he pulls out a horseshoe, braces one end of it on his leg and pulls it open.

I stood there laughing and shaking my head in disbelief. Partially because this was a feat of strength I had first read about not so long ago and couldn't believe it - plus here I was seeing it live in a hotel room in Morristown, New Jersey.

And partially because, while other people were entertaining themselves with gossip magazines, the Iron Tamer was entertaining himself with the willful destruction of horseshoes and nails.

He wrapped up a nail for me, handed it to me and told me how to position my arms. I pushed and wham! My biceps cramped up in both of my arms. I stretched my arms trying to make the cramping stop, shook it out and tried again.

"Now, I know you are strong enough to bend this" he said in his Tennessee accent.

They cramped up again. Ugh! This was going to have to wait a bit I guess. It was a shame because this was cool stuff and I wanted to do it! Oh well at least I could ask questions.

"Where did...blah, blah, blah..."

"When did...blah, blah, blah..."

"How did...blah, blah, blah..."

Dave interjected and told me about the Association of Oldetime Barbell and Strongman (AOBS for short) dinner in Newark, New Jersey.

"A lot of the active strongmen today are going to be there, you can go as my guest and meet them for yourself."

I was going to meet the strongmen! I could pick their brains and find out how they reached high levels of strength! This was my opportunity to ask some of the Supermen themselves how to get Kryptonian strength!

There I met many of the strongest people period - like my future mentor Greg Matonick, Chris Rider who would also become my coach, Sonny Barry, Mike Bruce, Stanless Steel, Dennis Rogers and Slim "the Hammer Man" Farman who was a protégé of the Mighty Atom and was his top student. These men knew the secrets and I wanted to learn them because they were onto something that others weren't. I would find out soon enough.

When Dave introduced me to Slim, I'll admit I wasn't fully aware of who Slim was, because I was still so new to everything. If you have ever met Slim, you know the second you talk to him that he is a big deal. Even though he's a tad up there in age (as I write this he's currently seventy-nine); Slim just has this presence about him that says this is a man to be respected. I also knew Dennis credited him as being a mentor and so does Dave. So when Slim looked at me and told me a couple words, I listened, because after all this man knows secrets.

"Son, did you know there is a power within you equal to every single person in this room...including myself?", Slim said, as he towered over me with a stare that is both powerful and knowing.

"In this room? I'm not so sure about that, Slim", I said laughingly as I looked around the room and saw a living collection of real life superheroes, just like the ones I had read about in the comic books as a kid.

"No, son, no, you are thinking about it the wrong way. You see, The Mighty Atom who taught me was even smaller than you and could do things that would blow your mind. You need to approach it like it's a matter of life or death for someone you love. It's all in the mind. That's the secret."

It's all in the mind, that's the secret. Apparently what separates Clark Kent from Superman is in the mind and not so much the muscle. Food for thought.

Slim is known as "the Hammer Man" for good reason. When it comes to levering sledgehammers, Slim is untouchable. He is known for levering two 24 lb. hammers on thirty-one inch handles. To get an idea of how hard this is, try lifting up a broom by the end of the handle. Now imagine that it were a 24 lb. sledgehammer. Quite a different story. On top of that, the hammers that Slim holds the record for aren't even the highest he has ever done. As I understand by people that know better, the number is in the 30s. I discovered how much of a legend Slim was after I had already met him. Like I said, I was brand new to all this.

After that conversation I got to witness the secrets live in action. I watched wrenches being bent, chains being broken and steel bars bent across the throat. Kids don't try that last one at home.

9

As it was time to leave, Dave said, "What did you think of all this?"

"I think I need to get stronger, a lot stronger, before I ever attempt any of these things, but at least I have a starting point. It's in the mind."

At that point I had something to start with. I knew it existed and I knew that the mental game was going to be huge part of it. I wanted to learn more.

I spent a bit of time getting generally as strong as I could. I had read that an exercise called the Turkish getup was used as a test of all around strength and that one with 100 lbs. would be a defining point of whether or not you are strong enough to become a strongman. So I trained with the getups and got to that level before I went to the next step.

I spent a bit of time trying to learn what I could on my own but instructional materials and Google can only take you so far. I needed a coach. I would find one later on but I had a lot happen in the meantime so for a while, that dream would have to be put on hold.

I felt as though there was something different about me, in a good way. I was happy but I longed for more. I don't really know exactly what it was, but I always felt as if I were destined for great things. At the time the future was unclear and to an extent it still is. I reach one milestone before finding the next one.

THE END OF ONE CHAPTER AND THE BEGINNING OF ANOTHER

In 2010, I was training to be stronger and I was getting stronger. I had posted a couple videos on YouTube of the things I was able to do. I was getting recognized and encouraged by some while others attempted to disparage me (there will always be some who spit on your accomplishments or accuse you of cheating).

All this was happening as I was en-route to getting married. I was married in mid-November 2010 to the girl I had loved for eight years. The following summer it felt as though someone flipped a switch and the love of my life, the girl who said she wanted to grow old with me, completely transformed into a different person.

I had dedicated myself to my marriage but no matter what I did it just wasn't enough. This girl who I had been in love with for years, who I felt would love me no matter what I did, suddenly hated everything about me, no matter what I did.

"Is everything ok between you two?" One of our concerned friends asked me in private.

"No. She won't talk to me. I don't know what to do", I said back to her. I was looking for answers and finding none.

I was trying everything and still failing. And let me tell you I was trying *everything.* Searching for answers - I even thought she might be possessed by a demon and threw holy water on her stuff. Yeah, it's funny to think about it now, but at the time I was desperate for anything.

Let me tell you also that whatever you think about demons or how you think you'll react - you don't realize who you really are 'til you hit your crucible. With this I didn't even fear for my own soul, my only thought was "Give me my wife back."

We were already in counseling per her idea and it still wasn't going well. I didn't know what was going on but I had this unease that fueled my suspicions. We were officially separated in late September - on the day after my 30th birthday. I decided in October to go back to the strongman dinner in what I figured would be a futile attempt to get my mind off of what was going on with my marriage.

I specifically remember driving down a particularly shady section of Newark and hoping someone might pull a gun or something on me. I even rolled down the windows of my car hoping someone would try something that would give me a good excuse to grab a hold of someone's arm and accelerate my car taking them with it and do horrible things. Needless to say, I was not in a good place. I went to the strongman dinner to get my mind off of it all and maybe try to have a good time, even though I knew it would probably be a lost cause.

I hadn't told Dave what was going on because I was trying to hide my pain from everyone, but he could tell there was something off about me. He just didn't know what it was.

So there I was. It was the Association of Oldetime Strongman and Barbell Association Annual Dinner and I was there...only I wasn't. My thoughts were elsewhere.

How can I keep my marriage together? No matter what I did it didn't seem to matter. I felt hopeless and lost and even though I would normally be excited to be in the presence of some of the strongest men in the world - only part of me was there. The other part was wondering what to do and what the next step in my life was going to be.

I was trying to hide the pain I was going through from everybody and I knew I was failing. I was failing at my marriage and I was failing to hide it. And with this being in the middle of the worst economic drop since the great depression, my personal training business was failing, too.

Put simply, I was a failure.

Amazingly some of the people I leaned on for support were my in-laws. They had reached out to me to try and tell me they didn't know what was going on with their daughter and it wasn't my fault like I had started believing.

"And the worst part of it is that I feel like even though all of these things I've done are failing. I feel like I am right on the cusp of something big. I can't explain it," I told them. If only she would have just hung in there she'd see.

But I was still depressed and not in a good place.

Once again, Slim was there. His wife Shirley had recently passed and he was feeling the pain. It was immediately visible to anyone who could see him. I felt a different kind of pain because my marriage was dead on arrival and I couldn't help but think it was somehow my fault, all my fault. I thought I was a good person, but just like anybody and everybody...I was far from perfect and still am.

To try to distract myself from the pain I figured seeing some amazing things from some of the strongest people out there might be of some benefit. And once again I saw some amazing things. Earlier that day I watched a guy named Chris "Wonder" Schoeck bend some steel bars...and he was my size.

As you already know, I found my way there by following the Iron Tamer David Whitley down the path of the strongman. I had looked to him for guidance for my path before and continued to do so now. He knew he was a bit of a guide and for whatever reason of all the trainers he knew, met and for whatever reason had forgotten...something made him remember me. I had no idea what it was.

Well, my thoughts wandered from the strength elite who I was in the presence of, to thoughts of my marriage. I wondered if it was probably dead on arrival. I no longer knew what the future held. The one constant that I always thought would be my future might not be. I sat there on the crossroads and wondered to myself.

"What's next?" I thought, "What do I do now?"

In a moment of serendipity, that is when I heard a gruff voice say to the right of me, "Would you want to learn the feats of strength and learn how to become a strongman?"

The voice belonged to a somewhat older gentleman - bearing a resemblance to Obi Wan Kenobi, if Obi Wan Kenobi was a bit beefier and looked like he was most at home riding around on a Harley. Here he was wearing jeans and a sleeveless t-shirt that had an illustration of a muscular man bending a heavy steel bar over his leg.

His arms bore tattoos of Frankenstein, of a Bowie style knife, of his wife's name and on his forearm it said "Strongman". On the back of the shirt was the saying "What's impossible to you is normal to us." It was the mantra of the strongman - what these people did was impossible...which is part of what drew me to it in the first place.

What these people knew differentiated Clark Kent from Superman. I would find out later that I was sitting face to face with Superman...and like Obi Wan Kenobi did for Luke Skywalker, he would drastically change the course of my life. His name was Greg Matonick and ABC News once referred to him as New Jersey's Superman.

He saw something in me that I didn't see in myself. This man knew secrets and he wanted to share them with me.

"I got instructional materials about the feats of strength the last time I was here but I never really got anywhere with them. I don't really know what else to do or where to start", I replied truthfully.

"I could teach you, I taught him." Greg gestured to Chris Schoeck who was seated at the same table as we were.

He was my size and bent some seriously intimidating steel bars earlier that day. He was the star of an in production documentary named "Bending Steel" which chronicled his time overcoming his personal shortcomings as he joined the real life supermen.

He looked at Chris and said to him, "Who taught you to bend steel?" fully knowing the answer. It was a rhetorical question that would change everything.

"You did," Chris replied, with a very serious look on his face.

Even though "Hairculese" Chris Rider, a big and immensely powerful strongman known for pulling trucks with his hair was the one who would later mentor Chris, Greg had started him on his journey and wanted to start mine.

I looked at Dave...I can't even be fully sure why but I suppose I was looking for direction from someone I looked up to and the one who showed me this path. Maybe I was wondering if this was really happening and looked to him for reassurance. The Iron Tamer looked me dead in the eye and gave me a single nod.

"Yes."

I'll be honest; I can't remember if I simply thought it or said it out loud but...

"Well, that guy is my size...and if you taught him and he can do that...then if you teach me and I work hard I'll be able to do the same thing."

"Well yeah, I'd love to learn from you. I'll be honest though I can't really afford to pay you much until my business is thriving."

You can't put a price on what he wanted to teach me anyways.

"I won't charge you nothing." Generosity that shouldn't have been given...especially considering how rare this skill was...and that he was one of the very few who could teach it. Maybe a hundred people in the world knew what he wanted to teach me, and even then, he learned through experiences that nobody else had.

"Well, where are you located?" I asked him.

"I live in Cinnaminson, New Jersey. It's south of here."

"You are in the state? Yes, I would love to learn how to be a strongman. Thank you for your willingness to teach me."

I was genuinely excited for the first time in a while. This would give me the glimmer of hope I needed to help pull me through the dark times. And dark times were ahead - that was for sure.

"The very first thing I want you to do is to buy The Mighty Atom's book. It's very hard to get anywhere without having read this book."

That book would become very special to me because it helped me get through some tough times and it would provide me with hope. If a premature boy born in poverty who was expected to die could go on to become something incredible, and then maybe I could, too.

As we were chatting and he was showing me pictures of his dog at the beach, I heard the dinner's emcee, the Mighty Stefan, announce Greg as an honored guest with the introductory line "Greg Matonick, who has never turned a would be strongman away." Several strongmen clapped. Many of them had gotten their start through him on their way - getting to where they are today.

This was going to represent a new chapter in my life and this was the man strong enough to lead the charge.

Later that evening, I happened to be in the lobby and saw a group around Slim, trying to make him feel better about the recent passing of his wife. I joined the group.

Now for whatever reason he looked right at me and asked me if I was married.

"Yes"

"Do you love her?"

"Yes"

"Do you ever fight with her?"

"Yes"

"Do you ever win?"

"No Slim, I don't."

I told Greg I would have to put learning how to be an old-time performing strongman on hold because I had something important to take care of first. I was nervous he was going to tell me it was now or never, but he said take all the time you need. I ordered the book and left there absolutely determined to hold my marriage together.

Even though I was separated I was going to find a way to make it work. I had to, no matter what it took. At the time I was working a side job as a brick-layer to help make ends meet while I was trying to hold my personal training business together. I worked like a dog to try to run both things at once while trying to fix all the problems I believed to have been caused by me. I did every single thing she asked, I jumped through every single hoop and no matter what I did, no matter how many times I said I was wrong, no matter how many steps I took forward - it still wasn't good enough. I carried it all on my shoulders. Luckily my shoulders were strong because I was going to need every ounce of strength that I had.

My cell rang and I knew what it was about even before I picked up the phone.

"Eric, are you sitting down?" my friend asked me. She was the wife of my best friend.

"Yeah," I said, my heart nervous and dreading what she was going to say, even though I already knew.

She asked me to come by so we could talk and comfort each other... face to face.

The news she told me confirmed both of our suspicions and would mean the definite end of it all. After this point, there was no point in trying to hold it together. It takes the strength of two to hold a relationship together and that was more than I could bare nor was willing to try any longer.

My now ex-wife was allegedly having an extramarital affair with my now former best friend. As of this writing, my ex-wife and the one who I thought was my best friend are currently married to each other. He never told me like a real man would. Instead she told me after everything was finalized - after the fact.

How could this happen? Two of the people I cared for and trusted the most. How could they betray me like this? I was devastated.

Not the kind of homicidal rage I thought might overtake me. It was more like my heart and soul was ripped out and I had lost all my strength.

All of the physical strength I had built up was gone and there I was lying in bed, crying, pathetic, unable to lift the sheets off me like I was a junkie going through withdrawal. Staring at the ceiling fan I thought about ending it all. What else did I have to live for?

I looked at the bedroom mirror and something called me to it. I didn't even have the strength to walk. I literally crawled from the bed to the mirror, using the dresser to pull myself up like I had been paralyzed from the waist down. I looked at the pathetic shell of a man staring back at me from the mirror in the eye and with a quivering voice I said.

"Eric, you are stronger than this. Don't let this kill you."

This was an affirmation that would help and would be a clue to the power of the subconscious mind. I would later discover how powerful these things could be.

I said it again and again 'til I regained enough of my strength to walk. I walked into the other room and noticed the Mighty Atom's book that Greg had told me to buy on my side table by my sofa and popped it open. I was immediately pulled into the book, despite what was going on, it gave me hope that if a baby born in poverty who was expected to die from the day he was born, could become one of, if not the world's greatest strongman, despite being smaller than me. There was hope that I wouldn't be a failure after all.

That book helped me through an incredibly dark period.

The dark times in your life are like the furnace that tempers the steel you are made from. We are all made from it, and newsflash...you are even stronger than steel. It is only during the dark of the night you might see the glow of a candle that would go unnoticed during the daytime. Go to the candle and use what little warmth it can provide until the daylight comes...and believe me the daylight will come. But before that, you must survive the night first.

The Mighty Atom's book was the candle. The warmth was the hope that I might be a strongman. My soon-to-be mentor was the light at the end of the tunnel.

The fact of the matter is you never know how strong you really are until your strength is tested. A true test of strength is harsh and when it is you can either give in to despair and let it crush you, or you can unleash your true power and understand what true strength is and overcome it.

This was a hard time, but it made me strong because there was also a glimmer of light that would get me through. This hope wasn't that I was just going to not be a failure, but I had the possibility to do something incredible. Something inspirational. I could be someone who can change lives. That would come later - I was still in a lot of pain because of what I was going through. Before I could help people get through their dark times, I had to finish going through mine first.

I did a lot of drinking. I was aware it was a crutch but in the meantime I needed to have it...just to help get me through. It's not something I would recommend to anyone but keep in mind I was still a weak shell of a man at that point. I just had hope for the future and it was only a short time that I needed it as I regained my composure.

And bit-by-bit, when I was having an okay day, I would read the book. If I were having a bad day I would drink. Slowly the good days outnumbered the bad ones and I was "okay".

I was surviving.

ENTER THE STRONGMAN

At the beginning of 2012, after going through the crucible, it was time to create a new identity for myself. I was no longer going to be Eric, "What's her name's other half." I was going to reinvent myself as Eric the strongman. In a sense every event that had transpired would set a course in motion for me to become a strongman, January 9th, 2012 marked my first day officially because that was my first day of learning how to become an old-time performing strongman directly from a strongman and I'll admit I had no idea what to expect.

Was this going to be like a crucible? Was he going to try to break me down physically and mentally like a drill sergeant would? How would I do? Would I really be able to do anything? Or was this going to be another disappointment? What should I bring?

I drove two hours and thirty minutes from my place to Cinnaminson where his place was and looked for "Atlas Welding."

The name "Atlas" was a throwback to Charles Atlas, the physical culturist who marketed the dynamic tension course and was popularized in the back of comic books.

The advertisement depicted a ninety pound weakling getting sand kicked in his face who starts exercising with the dynamic tension course; it makes him strong and muscular to stand up to the bully and walk away with the girl.

It was a very successful ad because a lot of people can relate in some way or another. The ninety pound weakling can be a metaphor for anything that prevents self-confidence. Even Charles Atlas' real name wasn't Charles

Atlas. But the titan that carried the world on his shoulders was strong. Greg liked the name because it was associated with strength and in his early strongman days he chose to go by the name "Greg Atlas" before simply using his real name.

I parked my car and found the door to the place but didn't find a doorbell. A bit nervous, but excited I breathed in and knocked. No answer.

I looked around the door to see if I could see a window or something just so I knew for sure because I was pretty nervous and didn't just want to barge on in. My excitement pushed through my discomfort and I opened the door anyways, stepped into the welding shop from outside in the cold, pulling it closed behind me.

A railing sat upon a workbench and he was grinding it down while wearing a thick fleece jacket (it was winter after all) and some protective eyewear. His helper was there wearing a similar sort of thing. Greg looked up at me, his future student.

Behind him was a wall adorned with pictures of some of the classic American muscle cars of the sixties and seventies and a bunch of pieces of metal, horseshoes and the like. On the far corner there was a door bearing several bible verses.

"Hey there, come on back," he said. "I'll show you around," as he led me through the door. "How was the drive down? Did you find the place ok?"

"Yeah. Before we get started I feel like I owe you an explanation about why I had to put you on hold because I think I owe you that. A short time before I met you I became legally separated from my wife. We are going through a divorce. I'm okay now but I wasn't then and I apologize for blowing you off," I told him.

"You know it's good you did that. So much of this is in the mind and if your mind isn't focused on it, you won't be able to do it. Come on in," he said reassuring me.

He led me to a door that had a sign hanging on it informing me that dreams would become a reality when you go through this door. It was right.

I walked through the door into the back of his metal shop.

He had a gym set up back there - well stocked for someone to develop some high levels of physical and mental strength.

The place was frigid. Freezing cold, like we had discovered an artifact in a cave that hid the secrets of the old-time strongmen. Old news to him but this was an exciting new frontier for me.

It was the perfect place for an upcoming strongman to learn the feats of strength and it had that mystical aura. He brought out a heater that resembled a jet engine and fired it up. It was loud like a jet engine would be but it blasted hot air out and heated the place up pretty quickly as he showed me around.

All along the walls were gnarled up pieces of metal with signatures and writing on them along with some of the strongmen who inspired him and the strongmen he taught. Literally there was mangled metal everywhere! It was awesome!

Traversing the gym was a chain going from wall to wall to wall. This was no ordinary chain though. The links on this chain were made up of spikes that he had bent with his hands into a "U" shape before welding the ends together. Literally hundreds of spikes would make up one length. On this chain hung various things he had bent. There was something that looked like a chandelier made up of horseshoes that he had ripped open. There were frying pans all rolled up and grouped together making it look like a banana tree. Believe me when I tell you this place was something else!

When you were here, you knew that this was no ordinary training space. It had a different kind of energy to it from all of the strongmen who had come and gone over the years, each one leaving their unique mark as a decoration of inspiration, all of this tucked away and hidden in the back of his welding shop in south Jersey.

Greg, knowing a thing or two about welding and metal work, had built a lot of the equipment he used to help him chase his dream of being a strongman. It reflected his influences, which were golden age bodybuilding mixed with *strongmanism*.

When Greg was a youngster, he had been picked on for his weight. Having felt powerless to stick up for himself at the time it gave him a lifelong fascination with anything strong and powerful. His arms were tattooed and one in particular would catch my eye. Frankenstein. Greg said he was his favorite monster because he was strong. Originally, Greg had turned to bodybuilding for strength because muscle was associated with strength and to Greg, the muscle would be the key factor. That's the way it started with me also.

Back during the golden age of bodybuilding it wasn't uncommon for bodybuilders to perform feats of strength. I remember seeing Franco Columbu blowing up a water bottle in the documentary "Pumping Iron" as an example of this. The bodybuilders before him were also reported to be all around strong and one bodybuilder in particular left an impression on Greg for being an all-around superhuman. That bodybuilder's name was John Grimek. As a bodybuilder had never been defeated in a contest and was a world class Olympic weight lifter competing at the Olympic Games in 1936 in Berlin.

While reading about John Grimek, Greg learned he had been a friend of The Mighty Atom and it was the Mighty Atom who inspired Greg to want to become a strongman. It was the Mighty Atom who pioneered many of the feats found in a strongman show today.

Some of the feats that the Mighty Atom was known for were biting through big steel nails with his teeth, snapping dog chains wrapped around his arm muscles, bursting heavy chains with the expansion of his chest, bending heavy iron rods with his fingers, making finger rings out of twenty penny nails, bending heavy iron bars by pulling on his hair with a special comb made out of iron, supporting the weight of a horse on his chest while lying on a bed of nails, driving a twenty penny spike through a two inch wooden plank with just one strike by hand, straightening out horseshoes and breaking them by hand, straightening out horseshoes with his teeth, resisting the pull of an airplane attempting to take off at one hundred fifty miles per hour BY HIS HAIR, changing the tires of a car without the use of tools, one arm snatching a dumbbell weighing one hundred and seventy-five pounds and more incredible feats. All of these feats were performed by a being who weighed less than one hundred fifty pounds, and had been told he would never reach his eighteenth birthday because he was too "fragile."

The Mighty Atom put new meaning behind the phrase "It's not the size of the dog in the fight, it's the size of the fight in the dog." He was not a "big dog" by any means, but man oh man the size of the fight in him was unfathomable and it led to some big things.

When Greg learned about the Mighty Atom, he figured that the most powerful thing was the mind and its command over the entire body. His approach was a mixture of the two, but the bodybuilding end of it was partially to "look the part of a strongman."

And here I was, the willing student standing in front of New Jersey's Superman. I stood there wide-eyed, uncertain and ready to learn the secrets that separated Superman from Clark Kent.

"So have you ever done any of the feats of strength before?" Greg asked.

"I've done Turkish getups with one hundred and six pounds and bent presses with one hundred fourteen pounds," I replied.

"How about bending steel?"

I nodded "No" as my answer.

He left the room and went into the front of the shop to grab some structural steel for me to bend. Measuring it out, cutting it to a predetermined length that he knew I would be able to handle before even knowing how much physical or mental strength I had.

He knew that based on his experiences with the strongmen who had crossed his path previously and knowing what the power of having a strong belief system can do.

He also knew it would be important that I see some success early on to build the confidence I would need to get that all important step of believing I am strong enough to bend steel and I would believe it because I already did it. It may have been an easier steel bar, but it was still a steel bar.

"I'm not going to demonstrate this because of my back, but I'm going to teach you how to bend this."

Greg had been in a car accident that was pretty severe and the injuries would have crippled or even killed an ordinary man. Greg was no ordinary man though and even though he seemed normal; when you got to know him you could tell he was in pain.

The fact that he was still able to walk, most of the time without the use of a cane, was pretty incredible but it made the thought of being a strongman a difficult one to grasp. That's why he stopped being a strongman but in order to keep *strongmanism* alive with himself and to the world, he wanted to teach the things he had learned over his thirty years of experience. I was one of the fortunate few who had this opportunity because I likely would have gotten nowhere without his help. This book is also intended to keep his name alive.

He pulled out a pair of shop rags like the ones you see mechanics use to wipe the grease off their hands. They were thin without much to them but they provide a teeny bit of cushioning, at least to get me through the beginning stages of being a strongman.

"Before you do anything, I want you to make sure your pockets are empty and the space around you is clear. You don't want to have any distractions around you because you want to be completely focused on what you are doing. Even though you don't realize it, these little things can distract your focus," Greg told me. I nodded in acknowledgement.

He hands the structural steel bar over to me and I hold it in my hands. This is steel, the kind they build buildings with. It's not supposed to be bent by anyone other than Superman.

"You need to believe that you are strong enough to bend this. Remember in the book about the Mighty Atom the power of the mind. Think that you are strong and you are strong. Set no limits upon yourself and you will have none. Set your mind to it and go like a bullet fired from the gun, once an action has begun it is done. Beginning and ending as if they are one."

I put the steel bar on the crook of my hip and tried to get into a good position. I closed my eyes and attempted the internal self-talk I thought I needed. I started pushing down on the steel and it started to move. I started to feel elation as the steel was caving into my strength. I lost the leverage on it and he stopped me.

"Ok, now readjust your position this way to get better leverage."

He adjusted my hands and the position of the steel bar so that I could put myself in a position to push down hard again. I pushed, once again it moved.

He showed me some new positions for it where I could continue to push or pull without my hands slipping off. I pushed, it moved, just like it had before.

When it came time to finish the bends he told me, "Okay now you put it on the floor and hold it down with your foot here, your hand here, and your other hand here. Set your mind on what you want to do, push that way and pull that way."

With elation and accomplishment I held up the finished product. It resembled a Jesus-fish but made out of steel, steel that I had bent into that shape, with my hands!

Then he brought out some nails that wouldn't be difficult to bend. They weren't strong enough to be a respected part of a show but for me they were a good place to start. The reason for this was the same reason he cut the steel to a certain length, because he knew it would be important that I see some success early on to build the confidence I needed. Who knows that they are tougher than nails?

The one who already bent them, of course.

And that man would soon become me. This nail went no problem and I was starting to get maybe a little over confident and he hands me another one. This one was different. I had a real hard time trying to bend this one. It still went, but I had a bit of work to do to become respected. That's okay. If it were easy then everyone would be doing it.

If it were easy, nobody would be impressed by it.

What a crazy way to start off the New Year and a new me! I felt like I had accomplished something of a dream. It was just the beginning, but what a beginning it was.

As I drove back home, I ached in a way I hadn't experienced in a long time. My hands were beat up, my forearm muscles were exhausted but I had my first bit of success and I was elated. Who knew I could do this stuff?

Greg knew, and I guess in some way I knew too. I doubt I would have traveled two plus hours if I thought I would never be able to do it. I knew it would be a shot worth taking.

Grabbing a bite to eat from either a convenience store or a Taco Bell (which one it was escapes me at the moment) on the way home I wished I could say what I was doing to anybody and everybody who would listen because I was proud to be doing it.

That would be the first of many treks I would do to his place.

A couple days later I went to my Toastmasters group. Toastmasters is a nonprofit organization that teaches people how to more effectively communicate. It's probably most famous for helping people with public speaking.

I originally joined because it was an inexpensive way to network to help me promote my personal training business and I hadn't been a member for very long. I had maybe a month or two of experience so I was new to the curriculum but it was a small group that I could communicate the importance of fitness or nutrition to and meet some people along the way. This time I wasn't going to talk about fitness or nutrition or anything like that. This time I brought the stuff I had bent with me and I was going to tell them anything was possible if they believed in themselves and put their mind to it.

It just seemed like the natural progression to talk about my new endeavor and seemed like a good fit for being a strongman.

I arrived earlier than the meeting started since I was coming straight from work. Today there was a brand new face. A blue eyed blond named "Elise." I smiled and introduced myself and told her about my training business and asked her about her business and the usual small talk that happens whenever you arrive early to a meeting. Turns out she had a business that involved sensory deprivation (floatation) tanks. If what she said was true then when the body's individual senses are cut off (light, sound, feeling etc.) then the brain can get true rest and operate on a different wave length. This could potentially be a higher form of meditation and I found it interesting because it was paralleling the path of becoming a strongman by learning the differences in the mind's control over everything we do.

As some of the other members walked into the room I knew we were going to get started soon so I opened up my bag and pulled the steel out that I had recently "fished."

"What's that?" she asked. Curiosity trumped her inherent shyness she had experienced prior to our meeting.

"It's a steel bar I bent into a fish shape with my hands," I said trying not to sound like I was bragging but yes, I was bragging.

"You bent this?"

"Yup," I smiled.

"No you didn't!" she said, smiling back with disbelief.

"Oh yes I did," smiling as I said it while I started pulling some of the other things I had bent. "Just wait till you hear my speech."

This could potentially be a turning point, not just for me but also for many people.

At this point, the meeting officially started. The gavel came down, the person in charge started, "Good evening toastmasters...yada, yada, yada." It was the same thing I had heard every other Tuesday thus far. Tonight would be different though.

I didn't have any speech preplanned or anything. I knew what I wanted to talk about and was just going to wing it and show some of the "props" I had brought to demonstrate that nothing was impossible.

I spoke with a new fire in my voice and came up with some of the things I still use to help people get through the tough times. You remember that bit where I talked about the candle in the night going unnoticed during the daylight? I came up with that during this speech.

The entire speech took a little over five minutes, which is the standard for where I was in the curriculum. I could have kept talking because the thing was putting itself together all on its own.

A couple days later I got a call on my cell from a number I didn't recognize.

"This is Eric from Eric Moss Fitness, how may I help you?"

"Hi Eric, this is Elise from the Toastmasters group. I'm not sure if you remember me, but I got your number from the contact sheets in Toastmasters. I hope it's ok that I called you."

"Hey Elise. Yes, it's cool that you called. What's up?"

"I enjoyed your speech the other day. You seemed really, really confident up there and I was wondering if you would be willing to mentor me. I think you would be really great at being a *motivational speaker*."

Hmm. I could be a motivational speaker? I had never really considered that before, but it seemed it would tie in well with being a strongman. What else would I talk about up there? How awesome I am? Who would want to hear that?

"Uhm, sure I'd be willing to mentor you, but I'll be honest, I'm not sure if I'm the best one for the task. I've only been a member of Toastmasters for maybe a month or two."

I can't remember how the rest of the conversation went but I did spend a short time mentoring her at the capacity that I could. What she didn't realize at the time was she put a seed in my head that would also change the course for things to come - because now I had gotten encouragement to be a motivational speaker.

Strongmanism and motivational speaking seemed like a perfect fit. One demonstrates, the other explains. But first, I needed to learn more about *strongmanism*. Luckily I had Greg to guide me.

Now that I had experienced my first bit of *strongmanism* and knew I was pretty good in front of an audience even though it was a small audience, I wanted to learn more and more and more and perfect my craft. This would give me new meaning that went beyond trying to learn some of the secrets of strength to apply to my personal training business. This would help me fulfill a couple of dreams at once.

Let's take a step back for a moment. I always felt that despite the things I had gone through as a kid, I was destined for great things. I wanted to be a star of some sort. I was fascinated with professional wrestling, watching promos of people like the Heartbreak kid Shawn Micheals, Triple H, Chris Jericho, The Rock, Mick Foley and Stone Cold Steve Austin. I loved watching them cut promos with the fire in their voice. When they were introduced onto the stage with their music playing, all eyes on them - I wondered what that must be like.

I was also fascinated with classic heavy metal - the likes of Ozzy Osbourne, Metallica, Iron Maiden and my favorite to this day Judas Priest. It wasn't just because I loved their music but also their stage presence. They could keep a crowd on its feet the entire time with seemingly a gesture and I would often dream of how amazing it would be to be in front of an audience and make them feel the same way I felt whenever they would play one of my favorite songs or shout out "What do you say New Jersey!"

All of this was before I really knew about *strongmanism* and ever toyed with the idea of motivational speaking. I knew I wanted to be in front of people, but never knew what my medium would be. Professional wrestling? I stand at a towering five foot seven inches and massive one hundred and fifty-three pounds and when I had tried to get myself around two hundred...well not all of it went straight to the guns and there isn't anything that can be done about height. Heavy metal singing? Even though I had developed the ability to hit notes only dogs can hear and dabbled in bands, the closest I ever got to performing live would be karaoke.

But *strongmanism* was a possibility and so was motivational speaking. The two of them fit like a horse and carriage.

The path to me was starting to become clear; I just didn't have the foresight to see it at the time but often as you walk through fog the path becomes clear as you go.

After I had a bit of success the previous week and knowing that I could do something in between the feats. My appetite was wet and I was hungry to learn more.

The next week I went down again and Greg raised the ante a little bit. This time we were moving onto steel scrolling. Steel scrolling is when you take a steel bar and bend it into a cool shape. It demonstrates control and allows for creativity in the strongman world. This was something that Greg enjoyed and I happen to love it too. Today he wanted to teach me a scroll called "the pretzel."

The pretzel is done by taking a piece of structural steel and bending it into a shape resembling the popular snack food.

Greg cut out a piece of structural steel that was the appropriate length and told me where to bend it. The way he taught it was simply doubling up what we had done the previous week. It is putting two of the steel fishes on the same bar so the tails faced each other.

A greater task is often done by simplifying it into smaller tasks. In this case, the pretzel is done by doing the fish scroll twice on the bar instead of one time. In doing so and keeping the bigger picture in mind, you can create something unique and different.

The next feat was a strongman classic, which is driving a nail through a board without a hammer. Basically you hold the nail in your hand and slam it down through the board in one strike. With this feat you only get one shot so you cannot hold back at all. There is a tremendous amount of fear associated with this one because of the danger of putting the nail through your hand; many people subconsciously hold back.

It's a great feat to use as a metaphor of pushing through barriers of fear, and I would later use it the following week to help Elise push through her fear. If someone could do this without fear…then standing up in front of a group of six people shouldn't be that bad either.

"Is there a particular feat that you'd really like to learn?" Greg asked me.

"I want to roll up frying pans," I said hopefully. I hadn't known it at the time but Greg had a different way of rolling up a frying pan than the other strongmen do. He showed me a couple positions to start the roll from and I opted to do it the same way he does. A teacher will always leave some mark on his student and my style would reflect his.

Even though the details for doing individual feats may change the principles carry over from feat to feat. It works like that with success in other areas too.

"Set your mind on what you want to do. Visualize it as if it has already been done, then let your body go through the motions like it's an instant replay."

Greg would have me read the pages out of the Mighty Atom's book that he had bookmarked for their importance to the stages I was in as an up and coming strongman. To him it was like a bible of *strongmanism*. Many of the passages he would read out loud to me as I attempted to hulk myself up.

Passages like:
"I am man. I am possessed of the Power. You are metal…without will. My will is superior to you. The Power will overcome you. You will bend…you will break." This was an affirmation the Mighty Atom said to himself.

Affirmations are a simple way you can influence your subconscious mind to break through self-limiting beliefs or negative thoughts. But they must be followed-up by focused, aggressive action. Affirmations without action are only a distraction. Like Greg told me, once you set something in your mind it's as if it's already done. You just have to make your body do what you mind commands.

From Greg's point of view, that book's importance to a would-be-strongman should never be overlooked; but even beyond the book Greg looked in many different places for strength information. Greg had subscriptions to the MILO Journal and numerous books, that are probably worth a bit of money because they are currently in demand, but beyond

Greg's hunger for strength books came his satisfaction of having experienced a lot of it himself. Experience teaches lessons that books cannot provide.

Trial and error can be a great learning experience but it takes a lot of time to be able to do it.

I would head to Greg's every weekend that I had the opportunity to go. The knowledge and wisdom I had gotten whenever I was around him was something that I feel I was blessed to receive. On top of that, Greg had become a good friend. Mr. Miyagi was more than a teacher to Daniel-san, and Mick was more than a coach to Rocky. Greg was more than a mentor to me.

The experiences with Greg blend together in my memories. It is hard to recall what experiences happened in what order, but the lessons are still there fresh in my mind.

I remember one time when I was working on a steel bar that I simply wasn't getting. Greg was brilliant when it came to knowing the steel and how much force it would take to bend it. Seeing me going at it and not coming through victorious, he wanted to test to see how much power I had. So he loaded up a barbell that was being held in place with chain to be able to put a number on it. He loaded it up with weight and told me to do barbell bench-press lockouts with it. He never told me how heavy it was.

I tensed up and he told me to relax. Save the power for the explosion. So I did and pressed it up without problem. He put more weight on the bar. I did the same thing no problem. He put more and more till he finally said.

"You definitely have the power here. It's your mind holding you back, nothing more." Basically when I was putting the steel bar in the bending position I was talking myself out of it before I even started.

How many times do we do that in our everyday life? And when I started pushing on it...I wasn't truly giving it everything I had. How many times do we do that with other things?

Another time I was working on a particularly tough scroll called "a loop." These provided difficult leverages to put power behind it and I was struggling with it.

"I'm going to leave you alone with this until you find the solution and get

33

it." He walked out of the gym and I guess went to work on a railing. I sat there. It was just me and the steel scroll that was half done. Incomplete. Because it was incomplete it sat there metaphorically laughing at me. It probably took me an hour or so and using one of the things lying around the gym was definitely tempting, but I abstained from using them and figured out how to do it.

There are always going to be problems with perplexing solutions and cheating can be very tempting. But those struggles can teach you things if you come out victorious.

Another time I was working on a very stubborn piece of steel. I had bent one similar to it previously without too much of a challenge and was starting to get frustrated that I couldn't do this one.

"Set your mind on what you are going to do and give it everything you got, irrevocable. Starting and ending the same, like a bullet fired from a gun," he said.

I pushed as hard as I could, no dice. I looked up at him looking for the solution.

"Again."

So I attempted it again while he watched me.

"You are stopping right before it bends, it won't always go at first, just hang in there. When you feel like you are giving it your all, just give it a little bit more. When you feel like giving up, just give it another couple seconds and it'll bend."

So I did. I remembered feeling like it wasn't going to bend, when I would normally stop pushing and instead of stopping I kept the pressure on and gave it more. It caved in. How many times in our life do we stop just before something happens?

"Now when you are ready," Greg said as he sat atop one of the stools in his workshop, propping one of his legs up, leaning on it with his elbow and interlocking his fingers in a relaxed manner as he spoke, "Send a press release to the newspapers and tell them you had just graduated so and so school for old-time performing strongmen. Just come up with a name of the school."

34

I sat there a moment bewildered.

"Greg, why don't I just tell them that I was your student? It's the truth after all, and I think it sounds cooler anyways."

The look he got on his face told me that thought had never crossed his mind.

"Well I guess I never really thought I had a big enough name to do that."

I was dumbfounded. Greg was a mainstay at the Association of Oldetime Barbell and Strongmen Dinner every year and had been announced as the one who would never turn away a would-be-strongman. Numerous strongmen say he was always willing to teach them and he was a large part of their success. How many before me did he reach out to? I'm not sure.

"Greg, your students are a who's who of performing strongmen."

He had been on ABC news once and was named by them "New Jersey's Superman." and here he was humbling himself. How could he not have a big enough name to be able to claim the things he had already done? And even then credit needs to be put where credit is due. Part of being a strongman is being truthful and another part is staying true to the roots of *strongmanism*.

Even on top of that and in my humble opinion, my story of being mentored by one of the greats is a great story in itself. The mentor-student relationship has been a central storyline in several movies like *Rocky*, *Star Wars*, and the *Karate Kid*. And this time I was living just like I was in a movie. Hey, maybe one day they'll make one.

With me going to Greg to learn as much as I could, every time I would go there it was always a long drive. While driving oftentimes my mind would go on autopilot, my thoughts would drift and I would day dream about the day to come. I would dream about what it would be like to actually perform on stage and I would come up with different ideas.

What if there was an actual school for strongmen? Or even a reality show? You take a bunch of average people, build them up, teach them the mindset, teach them the feats of strength, teach them the ins and outs of running a show, teach them how to get gigs...etc. I thought it might be a pretty cool idea.

And at the same time, Greg didn't have any strength prerequisites before taking on strongmen.

"Hey Greg, I had an idea on the way down here," and I told him about my idea.

"Even though the mindset can give someone who has never touched a weight before in their life the strength they need, it's much easier to do it with someone who has already lifted weights. It's not because their muscles are necessarily stronger, but because they've already built themselves up a certain amount and are going to be more confident in their own abilities going into a feat. Someone who lifts weights knows they are stronger than the average person."

As I continued going to Greg's gym I got stronger and stronger. He taught me auxiliary exercises that would get my wrists stronger and the reasoning he used is when you have strong wrists and hands, it gives you more confidence in the feat (a lot of feats require strength from the forearms down).

When you don't adequately prepare, you sabotage yourself. Not just because you are limiting the tools you have to use, but also because you also subconsciously set yourself up for failure.

And going down to Greg's we didn't even cover feats or mindset every weekend. I just liked being around him because he was a friend and also because you become like the people you associate yourself with. I like to associate with people who are all around good, successful and ethical people because that is who I wish to become.

They say you are the average of the five people you hang around with. Who do you hang around with? Are they going to push you forward or hold you back?

A good coach will push you forward and so will a good friend. When I went through my divorce there were only a few people who checked in on me. I used that as a filter of who my true friends were. The ones who checked in on me were there to help me through. The ones who didn't were only "friends" because I entertained them with my sense of humor, so on and so forth.

Greg was both a good friend and a good coach who would pick me up and push me forward to a better version of myself and it made me feel good to be around him. I intended to do the same thing for others.

And that is the greater purpose. Plus I wanted to eventually help Greg start a school for strongmen.

THE BEGINNINGS OF REBAR TO RIBBONS

Sometime in between my weekends with Greg, I knew that I wanted to be getting more training so I had picked up rebar (reinforcing bar) from a local Home Depot.

Rebar is what is put into concrete and roadways to give it tensile strength. It is meant to reinforce pavement to make it stronger. Having dealt with rebar as a bricklayer I was aware of how strong it was. I bought some of it simply to practice. Besides I couldn't just continue to bum steel off of Greg, he was already giving me so much by teaching me how to bend it and how to take charge of my mindset. He didn't need to supply it also.

I was getting ready to start preparing myself some dinner when I heard my cell phone ringing. It was from someone I care about but don't wish to mention her name. I'll just say they were really there for me when I was going through my dark time. I hadn't realized I would soon return the favor.

"Hi, Eric."

"Hey, what's up?"

"I have some news."

"What kind of news?"

"I'm alright." she said, not to get me worried, "but I went to the doctor and he found a lump and it is breast cancer."

A surge of many things hit me at once. But the first instinct I had was to try to give her inspiration, to tell her about the power of the human spirit which I was still learning.

"Listen, you are strong, the spirit inside you is strong...you can beat this I know you can. You need to believe me, you can beat this."

After trying to encourage her, I got off the phone and started shaking. I needed to bend something and I grabbed the first thing that I could find.

The closest thing was the rebar. Too short to be put into a fish shape but I instantly remembered the first steel fish I ever did and that sparked the inspiration for my Rebar to Ribbons Campaign. I figured if I did this, I could paint it different colors that represented different kinds of cancers and this would provide what could be the most important part of a person's battle - that glimmer of hope that inspires them to fight the good fight.

Rebar, originally meant to reinforce concrete, would now reinforce the human spirit by demonstrating that if it's stronger than this, maybe it's stronger than cancer too.

To this day the last I heard, she is in remission and I pray she stays that way.

When I next saw Greg, I told him about my idea for Rebar to Ribbons and he said that would be a great thing not just because of the practice I would get at bending things but it gives a great message of inner strength.

"You're going to need a grinder to take the sharp edges off," he said as he pulled one down off of the rack in his welding shop. He handed it to me.

"Here you go."

"Thank you...how much do I owe you for it?" I had guessed around $20. I was wrong.

"It's yours; you don't owe me anything for it."

"Here, take this," I said pulling a $20 bill from my pocket earnestly hoping he would take it.

"No, no, I want you to have it," he said, putting his hands up in the air like I had pulled a gun on him.

"Greg, you can't keep just giving me stuff for free like this," I said knowing he himself also had bills to pay and he had given me so much already.

"I can do anything I want and I want you to have this."

I knew to argue with him on this would be an exercise in futility. Even after he had given me so much of his time, his knowledge, wisdom and steel he was giving me this too. Greg was just like that. He liked to give and that's why he was the one who would never turn away someone who wanted to become a strongman.

He seemed to get great joy out of helping me any way he could, so I just looked at it and shook my head in disbelief as he brought out the accessory that I would need to change the grinding wheel. The man definitely was a giver.

"Thank you, Greg."

Greg's generosity was just one of many things he did. Rebar to Ribbons is really just a continuation of the things he had taught me about the power of the human spirit being able to conquer just about any of life's challenges.

He had also taught me about being what he called an all-around strongman. When he originally started talking to me about it I took it at face value of being good at multiple feats and not specializing in anything.

What he really meant was being an all-around strong person in life and especially being strong of heart. A strongman doesn't use his strength to make people feel inferior. A strongman uses his strength to help people.

This is what Greg did for me (I always say it took a strongman's strength to put me back on my feet) and it's also been the success behind several people. If you want to be treated well, try being nice first. If you want to be appreciated, try showing appreciation first. It's amazing how that happens.

My intention is for Rebar to Ribbons to be an extension of that - using my strength to help pull people through their tough times, where they can demonstrate their strength as well.

A while back I bumped into someone who is very active with Pancreatic Cancer awareness and knowing this I informed him about my Rebar to Ribbons project. Now if you aren't familiar with Pancreatic cancer, I'm not surprised because unfortunately it doesn't get very much attention in the press.

This fellow David (not David Whitley) who I met through a mutual friend had asked me for some ribbons to donate to the Pancreatic Cancer fundraiser known as Purple Stride. I donated my services as a strongman and brought ten ribbons with me to distribute to some of the people in attendance who were dealing or had dealt with it before.

One fellow I gave a ribbon was a survivor. Because pancreatic cancer has a single digit survival rate, that is no small accomplishment.

"Can I tell people I bent this?" he jokingly asked.

I looked him in the eye and told him, "You can tell people you survived pancreatic cancer. That's more impressive than any feat I ever did."

He stood there, surprised by my response I suppose, didn't say a word and shook my hand and nodded. I hope his story inspires people, because people need inspiration, especially during the darkest of times. They need to know - it's possible.

One of the things I try to impart to people when they talk to me about strength is "it's not about brute force." It is the ability to crush obstacles and break the chains of limiting beliefs. Strength is internal. It is the ability to withstand and the ability to overcome. It is the silencing of the internal voices that say you aren't strong enough, tall enough, smart enough or cool enough. Strength comes in many forms.

Steel is simply a metaphor for whatever someone might perceive as being *impossible*. The odds of surviving pancreatic cancer more than five years is six percent. Daunting odds. Terrifying odds. But survival is not impossible; if you can cling to hope and belief that you have the power within you to defeat it, maybe you can. And when you do, you can provide hope for someone else; if they know it can be beat it can inspire people.

The same is true for just about anything incredible.

THE FIRST TIME I BENT A STEEL BAR ON THE BRIDGE OF MY NOSE.

Going to Greg's gym every Sunday I was progressing very rapidly. I was a hungry student and he had the knowledge and experience from his career that was shortcutting the process. When you combine a good student and a good teacher, it provides a perfect storm and that's what we were.

I would listen intently to his words, telling me the power of the mind. Explaining all the stories of the legendary strongmen he would read about, had met and even some of them he had trained. He envisioned me being right up there with the legends. Though I had made great strides, I didn't see myself up there. However with him talking about it, the possibility was there at least.

"What I'd like you to do next is bend a steel bar with the bridge of your nose. That's an amazing feat of mind over matter and to me it epitomizes a strongman," he said.

Now I had seen Slim's video where he talked about bending reinforcing bar on the bridge of his nose. Slim talked about the sacrifices he had made to his health with that particular feat including shooting pains down his arm from crushing vertebrae in his neck and even losing vision in one of his eyes. I wasn't sure I wanted to make that sacrifice.

"Greg, I don't know if I really want to learn that feat. Slim did a lot of damage to himself. I don't know if I want to make that sacrifice," I told him.

"I understand," he said. "But keep in mind Slim is an old man at this point and had been doing that a long time." He started to walk out of the room to grab another piece of steel for me to bend into a scroll.

He paused and turned to face me.
"But if you do decide to do it, because there are so few who are willing to...it could put you up there with the top strongmen today. You could be one of the best," he added thoughtfully. I couldn't see his face because he was facing the other direction but he was likely grinning as he walked out of the room.

I slept on it, took about a week thinking about it and decided to go for it. "You know, just once I'd like to be one of the top guys in the world at something. Being one of the best strongmen would be AWESOME." I thought to myself.

I don't really know if Greg intentionally put a seed in my head. Knowing his knowledge of the power of affirmations, incantations and the mindset and knowing me, the impressionable student. Now that I write this, I suspect he knew exactly what he was doing, and I thank him tremendously for that.

I went back the next week with clarity and purpose. I was going to learn how to bend steel with the bridge of my nose.

"Hey Greg, I changed my mind about the nose bend. I want to do it. Just once I'd like to be great at something," I told him.

"I'm very happy to hear you say that, Eric. It's one of my favorite feats because it demonstrates mind over matter and is everything about being an old-time strongman." I hadn't realized it at the time but it was also a bit of a rite of passage for Greg to have me do this.

With structural steel there is a coating called "mill scale" on the surface. When steel is bent, the scale flakes off unless it is wire brushed off first. When a steel bar is bent over the leg it's not a big deal to have mill scale flakes get on you. When it's near your eyes the rules change and special attention has to be made so the flakes don't go into your eyes. Often times after people meet me after a show, they ask me what those flakes are on my shoulders. That's what the flakes are.

So Greg cuts the piece of steel and wraps a shop rag around it nice and tight to make sure nothing gets in my eyes and leans the steel bar on a piece of gym equipment nearby to explain the "technique" behind bending a piece of steel with your nose.

He places his finger on the bridge of my nose between my eyes. "Have you ever seen that party trick where you can stop someone with just one finger by pushing against the bridge of their nose? This is where you are going to bend the steel and that's what makes it so amazing to the audience. You are going to face upward and pull the bar straight down into the bone of your nose. It's stronger than most people think."

Ok, let's do this. I get the bar into the position he just described.

"Now set your mind on what you are going to do, clear it of everything else. And just go through the motions as if it's already happened."

I give a quick internal affirmation to myself as I breathe deeply pushing out all negative thoughts.

"I know that this is going to hurt and I'm ok with that because I know it's not going to kill me. No matter how much it hurts. No matter how much my body says stop. I'm going to pull as hard as I can no matter what."

I pull hard. I can feel the pressure on my nose building and I feel my arms moving downwards. It was bending but even though it was bending I could still feel myself not quite giving it my all. It bends to the point where I lose leverage on the bar.

"Oh my God! You did it on the first try. That's very good," he said, the proud teacher.

"Now, what you do is you hook your wrist around the bar like this so you can get a bit more space for leverage."

I pull again and it bends a little bit farther and I finish the rest with my hands.

"That's it, it's official," he told me. "You're an old-time strongman." He says throwing me a shirt. It was a black shirt with a picture of a muscular man bending a steel bar on his leg. It's the same kind he would proudly wear and it had the following words written on it.

"Steel bending strongman. What's impossible to you is normal for us."

I was happy as anything because I had done something that so few are able to do. I shouldn't say they aren't able to do it. You *can* do it...but *"will* you do it?" is the real question.

He looked at me with pride. "I'm very impressed you got that on your first try. I knew you would get it but I didn't think it would be today. I've never seen anyone get that on their first try," he told me.

I was proud but I also felt a bit guilty.

"Greg, I could still feel myself holding back though. I know it still went but I could still feel myself holding back," I told him.

"I know you did. It's normal because we have this instinct for self-preservation. Your body was trying to tell you to stop but you pushed yourself past it and when you can go there you can continue to go there a little bit further each time. Each time you push yourself past it you are able to take it to the next level. And who knows where the end is but in your own mind," he said, leaning back on a piece of equipment and letting me in on his wisdom.

Like I said, this is the strongman who knows the secrets that separate Clark Kent from Superman.

BENDING A WRENCH FOR COPS AFTER TOTALING MY CAR

I was becoming a strongman and I was a bachelor.

For being relatively new at being a bachelor, I wasn't doing too badly for myself. Girls were interested and I was getting plenty of dates. I'd check my email and see I had new message on the online dating site I was using at the time so I'd go check it.

Wow, this girl took her time. Anybody who knows me knows I can get a bit chatty at times and that was reflected on my profile. This girl obviously read it (good for her she can actually finish something she starts) and had responded to all my little jokes I'd put in there. This one was obviously well thought through.

I go onto her profile and see that she is a mixed martial arts instructor who lives in Princeton, which is a bit far out of the way to be traveling on a regular basis. But hey, I was traveling through Princeton every weekend on my way to Greg's place; this would simply be a stopover. And besides, if someone is worth it then they are worth making the trip for. Only one way to find out if she was worth it.

So we set up the date. It was going to be on a Sunday night on the way back from my mentor's place and we would walk around Princeton. I packed a bag because I would have to get changed at Greg's gym, so I could arrive at the date a sharp-dressed man.

While I was at Greg's gym I bent a steel bar on the bridge of my nose to capture it on film. Greg knew I had a date and he had other stuff he needed to do anyways, so we called it a bit earlier than usual and I got changed and headed on out.

I got on my blue tooth headset and talked to a friend of mine excited about my date. I came up over a hill and bam!

The next thing I knew I was staring at a deployed airbag with my buddy screaming, beckoning me to answer him.

"Eric, are you okay? Eric, can you hear me? Are you there? Can you hear me? Are you okay?"

"Yeah...yeah I can hear you. I think I just had a car accident. I seem to be okay though," I said in a bit of confusion. "Let me check on the other person."

The other person was behaving like a maniac. While I'm trying to call for help she's screaming in my other ear and after enough of that I told her to please be quiet. Except, I wasn't nearly that polite.

I call my date to tell her I wasn't going to make it because I was just in a car accident (a reasonable excuse to cancel as any out there really). I call my parents to tell them what happened also. They took it rather well.

The police arrive on the scene checking on the maniac and me. They section it off and do all the necessary work that police do in those situations. They also let me know that this is a shady area and the reason the person acted like a maniac when I checked on her was because she was recently beaten and mugged in that very same town. I guess she assumed I was going to do the same thing.

Okay, she's forgiven.

Now they don't think I should stick around the area because it's dangerous so they offer to take me to a gas station in the next town where I can wait for my ride home.

"Just get everything you need and we'll take you on over."

So I grab my 'go-bag.' My go-bag is filled with my strongman stuff. Spikes, wrenches, drill bits, horseshoes and a couple other various odds and ends, not really typical of what you might find in a typical 'go-bag' but hey there is nothing typical about a strongman to begin with.

"Before we allow you into our vehicle, I need to check your bag to make sure you aren't carrying any weapons."

Perfectly reasonable but this should be interesting. I hand him the bag.

"What the hell is all this?"

"I bend those."

"What?"

"I bend those."

"I'm not sure I understand. What do you mean you bend those?"

"I'm training to be a professional old-time performing strongman and I was heading back from my mentor's place. I would bend those as part of a show. Right now I use them for training 'til I'm ready to do a show."

"Wow, that's really cool"

"Thank you, I appreciate that."

So the two officers are asking me questions about it on the drive over to the gas station where I was going to be picked up.

When we arrived, "You want to see me bend something don't you?" I said grinning.

"Well you indicated in the report that you felt something in your thumbs."
"Forget my thumbs, I'm fine. You want to see me bend something?"

"Yeah I'd love to," one of them said.

"Grab all your cop buddies; you're going to get a free show."

So there I was, in a dress shirt and blue jeans, reaching into a bag to grab a wrench, in the middle of a gas station, an hour after totaling my car, bending a wrench for the cops who picked me up. Why? Because, you know, that's the sort of thing I do.

I must have had a ton of adrenaline in my system because that wrench folded up easier than any wrench I've ever done before or even since I've written this. Wrenches can be tough sons of bitches sometimes. Not this one though. This one put up no fight at all.

After they left, while I was waiting for my ride, I called my date to kill some time figuring she had no plans this evening (because I was her plans and had to cancel...for a perfectly legitimate reason). She ended up making the trip over to hang out with me because it was only 10 minutes away.

Wow, I was impressed. But should we really count this as our first date? A gas station? Good place to bend a wrench for some cops who picked me up an hour after totaling my car, but it's not exactly the most romantic thing to take a girl to. Oh well, it was nice meeting her and it was a thoughtful gesture. We'll figure out something for the next time.

As I lay in bed that night I reflected upon my day and I started laughing at myself for being a cartoon character. I thought, one day this'll have to go into a book (and it just did).

THAT ONE TIME I GAVE MY AUTOGRAPH TO A PLAYBOY COVER GIRL

I was sleeping when my cell told me I had a text message. It was the girl who met me at the gas station after I bent the wrench for those cops. I had a date with her that night and she was canceling our date. Blowing off all future dates since she thought we weren't a good fit. Bummer because I thought we were getting along great.

After I thought about it my mind started dwelling on why she would cancel our date. This girl had gone to great lengths to date me from the first message on the dating site to actually meeting me at the gas station when I had to cancel our first date because I was in a car accident (really, is there any more valid excuse than that?)

Later on when I would replay the events of why she would think that, I started to connect the dots and realize she wanted mostly "fun" and I hadn't picked up on the signals. If you think I'm making this up, I already ran the scenario and the clues past some of my friends who are girls and they all agreed, yeah I didn't pick up the clues, and they were really obvious.

Apparently her joke about us skipping the normal steps of dating and getting straight to business with her in the back of a car after her friends left right in the parking lot of the bar we were in wasn't a joke after all. Oh well.

Anyways, suddenly my plans are free that evening. No sense in feeling sorry for myself. Another one of my friends had asked if I wanted to go meet former WWE Diva and Playboy Cover Girl Ashley Massaro earlier that week and I told him I already had plans.

Ashley Massaro was the winner of the WWE Diva search that was popular a while back. From there she was asked to pose for the April 2007 issue of *Playboy Magazine* and appeared on the cover. She had this punk/skater/school girl vibe. That day, she was wearing a short skirt, fishnet leggings and a backwards hat. She carried a skateboard with her though I've never seen her ride one. The look and the skateboard are likely simply part of her "brand."

My buddy, Joey, who told me about this was friends with the bar owner where she was booked to do a meet and greet and texted me one last time to check to see if I wanted to go. This time, I actually was available.

"Think I could bring a frying pan?" I asked.

"If you can get it past security."

"Oh I'll get it past security," I promised.

I showered up, carpooled with my friend and we met up with some of his other friends there. I pulled the frying pan out of the bag.

"What's the frying pan for?" one of his friends asks me.

"I'm going to roll this up, sign it and give it to her. She'll never see it coming. It'll be funny."

I gave him the rundown of being a strongman and talked about some of the things I had already done, like the time I bent the wrench for those cops an hour after totaling my car. Some of them were familiar with me and what I do but hadn't really seen it live.

This was going to be fun.

We planned it out in advance that my buddy Joey was going to record the whole thing as it unfolded. We were sitting at the bar and one of the guys in the group saw her walk in and says, "DAMN!" Yeah, she was a looker that's for sure.

We all get in line to buy the required picture for her to autograph and wait our turn. I try to keep attention off the frying pan just to avoid any annoying security guards that might be looking after her. No need for unnecessary attention...yet.

"We're up soon, are you ready?" I asked him. I only really had one shot for this and I wanted to make sure it was captured.

He laughed, "Are you ready?"

"Oh yeah, this is going to be good."

It was my turn.

"Well, hey honey, what's your name?" she asks so she knows what name to sign on the picture without even looking up at me.

"Eric Moss and I have a surprise for you."

"Really? Well, I'm excited!" she said. "Oh honey, not nearly as excited as you are going to be," I thought to myself.

I waited for her to finish signing the picture and asked, "Are you ready for your surprise?"

"Yes," she said standing up out of her chair looking up at me.

I point down at the frying pan which was level with my crotch. As an aside, I wonder how many people claim to have a surprise while pointing down in that general direction.

Never the less, I put my hand on the pan and start crushing it down, rolling it up in plain vision for her to see what I'm doing.

"HOLY COW! LOOK! LOOK!" She exclaimed.

She nudged her manager while he was trying to order food from the bar. By the time he stopped what he was doing I was finished rolling it up and she was clapping.

"Wow! Impressive! Very cool!" she says moving towards me. I pull out my silver sharpie and look her in the eye smiling, knowing I was about to turn the tables.

"Now I'm going to autograph this...for YOU!" My friends burst out laughing as I start writing while she stared at me with disbelief.

Afterwards we needed to move along so she could sign other people's autographs and head back to the bar. Had a couple more beers, joked around and her time was over. She headed outside to have a cigarette. Ugh, smoking is not hot. Oh well.

I walked outside on the pretense that I didn't know she was out there and was getting a breath of fresh air. I walked outside, took a sniff of the spring air and turned around. She smiled and waved.

"What is this, your entourage?" I said, gesturing to the people around her while laughing. I'm not sure what I thought was funny.

"It's ok you can come over here," she said inviting me to come closer so she could ask me about how I do the things that I do.

I had recently taken a video on my phone of me in Greg's gym bending a steel bar on my nose while he guides me through words and showed it to her.

"That's amazing, how do you do it?"

I did what I could to explain it.

"Have you ever heard those stories where a mother, who had never touched a weight in her life, could lift a car off of her child to save them. She could do that because there is nothing holding her back. She has no time to talk herself out of it which is something that we all do."

"So it's in the mind? Like karate or something?"

"Uh, yeah, something like that I guess."

That happened, I believe on a Saturday, and I can't remember how I told Greg about it. I just listen for opportunities to do unique things when they present themselves.

It was simply a time to cross a fun thing off a bucket list that I don't have and would make for a fun story to tell one day.

And the girl from Princeton, it likely wouldn't have worked out anyways.

MY FIRST TIME PERFORMING FOR A LARGE AUDIENCE AND BEING ASKED TO JOIN THE CIRCUS

"Dude you should come to this costume festival in the city that I'm going to with some of my friends. They have a lot of side show stuff and there will be a lot of girls there. They'll eat your strongman stuff up with a spoon."

Sounded good to me. I could use the experience and exposure after all. At the time, I was toying with using "Hercules of Hopatcong" as my stage name and I still had a store-bought Hercules costume leftover from Halloween.

My friends had taken to calling me Hercules for a while after that chanting "Hercules, Hercules, Hercules" clapping in tribute to the Nutty Professor every time I walked in a room.

So I packed up my bags to get changed and put two frying pans in the bag I'd walk in with. I wasn't fully sure how I'd get this past security but hey it's nothing I haven't done before.

I walked around kind of taking it all in and didn't see any girls I fancied. I drank in all the oddities I saw and awaited my turn.

"Dude, they are gathering people up for the talent show. Time to go backstage."

I handed him my flip-cam and said, "Make sure you capture this on film." I neglected to tell him that I was going to roll up two frying pans into each other as I went backstage.

As I was sitting there, it felt surreal, as I looked at the others in their weird costumes. Knowing the sorts of things you might see in an old-time Vaudeville show and knowing that the Mighty Atom would wear a leopard print tunic...this must have been what it would have been like back then. I started chatting it up with two seemingly normal guys back there with me who were going to do a comedy routine.

"What do you do?" they asked.

"I'm a strongman," I replied being purposefully cryptic.

"Huh?"

"You'll see," I grinned.

I walked out when I heard my introduction called and a guy dressed up as a demon asked me over the microphone what I was going to do. I announced I was going to do a routine called "Double the Pan Damage" in a bit of mocking reference to a promotion for some Jean Claude Van Dam movies on television. I don't think anyone got my joke that night.

I gazed out at the audience. It's weird when you look at a big crowd (in this case 500 people) because they don't look like people. I'm not entirely sure why, but people look like cardboard cut outs that move around. I guess it's kind of like when you look at a cityscape from far away. It looks two-dimensional.

"Double the Pan Damage! Double the Pan Damage!" he belted out rousing up the crowd. "DJ, let's pick up some music!"

The music came on...I don't even know how to describe the music...but let's just say it was a far cry from Judas Priest. Oh well, it was what it was. I banged the frying pans together a couple times so that everyone could hear it and tossed the larger of the two on the floor of the stage.

Now it was time to go through the motions which I had been trained to do. Put the frying pan in the bending position and crush down on it rolling it up in. The crowd started screaming.

"Oh wow, he's got some power there." I heard over the loudspeaker. No time to waste because I knew I didn't have very long up there. I grabbed the second frying pan and proceeded to roll it around the first one. Actually right then and there was the first time I had rolled up two frying pans into each other. I knew from rolling up frying pans before that I would be able to do it no problem...assuming I didn't choke but hey, I wasn't paid to be there so whatever. I was doing it for the experience of being on a big stage. I heard someone yell, "You're amazing!" and I'm beyond amped up as I finish 'Double the Pan Damage' and hold it up while flashing the metal symbol and triumphantly yelling, "YEAH!". Metal for life \m/.

After my act was some weird interpretive dance numbers. Weird like "snails having sex." Would you believe that was the one that took home the grand prize? The grand prize is returning next year free of charge. Uhm, they can keep it.

I got my flip-cam back and decided to walk around to start gaming any of the girls who had seen and screamed for me on stage. Once again nobody really tickled my fancy but I still wanted to get feedback from strangers.

One of the guys I was with took it upon himself to wing for me, but I guess he didn't really know my type. I'm slightly less than average height for a guy and don't like it when girls are taller than me...or when they are strange. He saw a girl who was strange, tall and looking my direction and introduced me to her. Not interested but maybe I can get some feedback; let's see if she saw the show.

She didn't. Turns out she was an artist, saw my frying pans rolled up and thought it was beautiful and that I could possibly make artistic purses.

What? Artistic purses? I'll never understand some people.

I walked over to one of the bars and ordered myself a beer and the guy next to me said, "You're one of us."

"Huh?"

"You're one of us."

"One of what?"

"I'm a musician with the Big Apple Circus. I can tell that you could have a good future with us," as he hands me his business card. I guess it isn't every day you get the opportunity to run away with the circus like everyone jokes about doing. I wasn't tied down to anybody at that point in time so this, I guess, would have been my opportunity. I didn't want to leave my training business behind though. It doesn't matter because I lost his business card anyways besides, I didn't fancy myself a carny.

Actually from what I gather, Big Apple Circus is a great operation.

Afterwards as the night got later, it got stranger and I headed for the comfort zone of the group I came with. I looked around for my friend who I came in with and a guy got right in front of me and asked me, "What the hell are you still doing with your costume on man...get naked!"

Uhm, okay time to leave.

"Get the HELL away from me," I declared. That made me EXTREMELY uncomfortable if you catch my drift.

I found my friend, jokingly told him about my experience, gathered up the troops and got the hell out of dodge.

It was an interesting experience to say the least and it got my feet wet and let me know, in a relatively low stress stage situation, that when it came down to it I wasn't going to choke in front of a crowd. Good news because I was planning on having some pretty big crowds in the future.

They were going to be a different sort of crowd though.

TWO SITUATIONS THAT ALMOST WENT SOUR
ON KARAOKE NIGHT

At one point while I was in Greg's gym, we were talking about what I should and shouldn't wear when I do a strongman show. Knowing that I had a relatively low level of body fat with visible ab definition and my shoulder to waist ratio had a decent proportion to them; I had suggested maybe doing it without wearing a shirt like I had seen in the promotional photographs of some of the old-time strongmen in the pre-vaudeville era.

"Now you don't want to do that because the guys might dislike you for that."

"Huh?" I was a bit puzzled with this one.

"You see, strength hits guys in a very primal area of their brain. Strength used to be the difference maker of the men before we were civilized. When guys see your strength, most of the time they will be inspired and enjoy it. Some of them may dislike you because they can't do it themselves. If you aren't wearing a shirt it'll look too much like you are simply showing off and that will set them over the edge."

Not the most encouraging words but...

"You know my assistant? He doesn't like Chris Schoeck."

I sat there listening.

"You see he is bigger than Chris, but Chris is much stronger." I already knew this because Chris is immensely powerful but I didn't know he didn't like him. Later on his assistant told me there is something about Chris that just rubs him the wrong way.

"Right now, Chris is stronger than you are but there are two ways of approaching it. You can either use it to inspire you or you can try to justify it in your head that he's cheating or that it's fake."

"Yeah that's what I thought when you originally offered to teach me. Chris is my size and therefore if he can do it, I can do it with hard work and your guidance."

"Yes, and you already knew that what he was doing was real. That's also why you should show some muscle by wearing a short sleeve shirt so it doesn't look fake."

Greg walked over to one of the walls of his gym in the section where he had Slim the Hammer Man's photos and some of the steel bars he had bent.

"You notice Slim in this picture? His arms are muscular, so you know he's really doing that. If you don't have any muscles and it looks like a breeze might blow you away, even though it's real it'll look like it's fake. Most people don't know that the mind is the more important part of this."

Food for thought. People not being able to justify something in their heads and using it as fodder to dislike me. I guess that comes with the territory.

Like many things I learned, I would see this lesson first hand in reality now that I'd became aware of it. You remember how earlier I said I enjoy singing karaoke? Well, here's a story of one Friday night.

I went to a place I sometimes go on Friday night because I know the Karaoke DJ carries some of my favorite heavy metal songs. I get to pretend I'm a rock star for the evening even though I'm reading it on the screen and have essentially no command of the audience though if I told them to drink more beer they probably would. And they do tend to cheer when I hit the high notes.

So I walk into the bar and I'm saying my hellos to the DJ and ask him to put in a song for me.

"Moss?" I heard a voice behind me say.

"Yeah?" I said as I turned around, my eyes attempting to focus on who this person was. He was visibly intoxicated. Suddenly I recognized him, "Hey Dan! It took a moment for me to recognize who you were. What's up? How have you been?"

He was the younger brother of a kid I was a great friend with when I was younger. It had probably been about fourteen years since I'd seen him. And a lot can change in fourteen years.

We sat down and he told me about the things he had been up to.

"Well, I was on the police force over in the Denville (a town nearby) but I got caught, with a DWI, so I was forced to resign my position over there and right now I'm between jobs as a contractor. It sucks man."

He was caught with a DWI and was again visibly drunk and slurring his speech again. I hoped he hadn't driven here.

"Whoa dude, bummer that happened."

"What have you been up to?"

"Well, I opened up a personal training business over in Parsippany. We are growing, not as fast as I'd like, but progress is progress and I've also become an old-time performing strongman."

He looked at me with a puzzled look on his face.

"Here, check out this video on my phone."

Normally I keep a promotional video on my phone showing some of the my feats of strength including a double frying pan roll up, double kettlebell bent press, steel bars bent on the nose and a couple others. The first feat shown was a double frying pan roll up.

"Can you bend a bottle cap backwards?" He asks without watching the rest of the video.

"I've never done it before but I probably could."

I watched The Man of Steel Sonny Barry do five of them in a row with one hand at the Association of Oldetime Barbell and Strongmen Reunion Dinner. If he can do that with one hand I'm sure I could do it with two.

I play along and ask him how he wants me to position my thumbs and he shows me. So following the directions, I push and it goes in and I figure on finishing it off with one hand like I'm pinching it down between my pointer finger and my thumb.

When he saw this he accused me of cheating.

"You're cheating! You aren't doing it right!"

At this point my buddy Stavros walked in and quietly had a seat. Stavros is a friend of mine who is not known for being the quiet sort. He's a boisterous Greek who had gotten compliments from Schwarzenegger himself on having the sort of physique that would make a great power lifter. Stavros saw the things I do in person, so he knows I'm legit. The bartenders know Stavros because he's the type that brings laughter into the bar every time and they give him his usual drink without him even asking for it.

"Pfft, the strongman can't even bend a bottle cap backwards!" he yelled sarcastically in the bar making a scene. He demanded that I go get a frying pan from the car to roll it up.

I told him, "No"

"Why not?" he said.

"Because I'm not your dancing monkey. You want to see me do it? Pay me or come to one of my prescheduled charity shows. I have three coming up within the month."

"He probably uses rubber frying pans!" he announces out loud.

Now one thing, we strongmen take our craft very seriously. There are a lot of people who mask themselves as one of us by faking certain feats and legitimacy is very important to our reputation. Legitimacy is everything to us and we don't take to being called a fake or phony very well. So my patience was starting to dissipate at a rapid rate.

At this point, he gathered a bunch of bottle caps and proceeded to bend them backwards and tried to throw them into people's drinks, including

Stavros'. This was getting out of hand.

I motioned for him to lean in closer, "Dude, you are acting like an a' hole, knock it the f' off."

"I don't care!" he yelled defiantly back at me. Well he was going to care when this 'fake' strongman loses his patience and slaps him around. My patience has its limits, my strength maybe not so much and I'd already had an argument with my girl earlier that evening so my patience was already wearing thin. Oh crap, I was going to have to slap him around a bit; someone who I thought was my friend.

Just then I heard my name announced on the PA system. "And now we have our resident metal singer Eric Moss singing Electric Eye, let's hear it for Eric Moss!"

Oh geeze, what timing, he is going to heckle me for sure.

The song Electric Eye by Judas Priest has a bit of a lengthy introduction so I went up to the microphone and waited for him to leave. He got up and left. Oh good, maybe I won't be taken away in handcuffs tonight after all.

After I dissipated some of my nervous energy that the situation had built up by singing one of my favorite tunes I sat back down with Stavros and ordered another beer.

"Dude! What the hell was that?" Stavros inquired in a laughing sort of way in an attempt to put me in a good mood.

"He was an old friend of mine from when I was a kid. I guess his life has gone down the toilet recently and when I showed him the things I've been up to, he didn't react to well to it." I shrugged my shoulders and took a swig of my beer.

Dan walked back in.

"Oh geeze, he's back," I said to Stavros.

Now where we were seated was the corner of the bar near the cash register was, so this next part probably had nothing to do with us.

Dan walked over to where we were seated and lunged between Stavros and myself to try to kiss the bartender who was trying to run a busy bar and ring up someone's tab.

Female bartenders don't like it when guys do that and heterosexual males like it even less. Dan is lucky that Cory the bartender didn't take a swing at him himself.

"I'm going to head out now, it was good seeing you again."

It was good seeing me again? Really? He extended his hand to say goodbye before leaving. I took it and squeezed his hand to keep him captive for a moment.

"You aren't driving are you?" I said. No way he should be behind a wheel in this state. He already had gotten in trouble for it once already anyways.

"No I'm staying with a friend a couple blocks over; he's waiting for me in the parking lot."

"Good, get your life back together." I released his hand so that he could leave and so that I could go and actually have a good time.

Right after he was out the door the bartender said to us, "He showed up like that, I only served him one drink. He gave me a one hundred dollar bill as a tip, so I went out to get him before he left. That's why he tried to kiss me. He's lucky I didn't knock him out."

"You and I both dude, he'd accused me of being a fake. Strongmen don't take kindly to that sort of thing because we take our craft very, very seriously. He had a ride, right?"

"Yeah, he's not driving, otherwise that would make us liable."

As his anger cooled about the situation, we continued talking. Inevitably it led to me talking about being a strongman, which he already knew. Now he'd gotten in trouble for alcohol problems as well, but the stuff that I do didn't threaten him on a primal level. Maybe because his life was in order (he was working as a bartender in a bar that was hopping and he was doing a pretty good job of managing it as well). Success in areas may present a threat to some, but not all.

I saw this quote a short time ago from David "The Iron Tamer" Whitley, the strongman who had introduced me to Greg.

"If you believe so strongly in your own self-imposed limitation that you insist on projecting it onto others, look elsewhere for a recipient. I have zero obligation to accept your limitation simply because you do."

Unfortunately Dan and I never got to talk it out and he's no longer with us. Dan if you can read this, I hope you can see I'm real and I hope you're proud to be my friend. I'll see you on the other side. Dan wasn't a bad guy, he was just having a bad night and I feel partially responsible for this.

Let your success be your success. Some will revel in it; some may be threatened by it, but oftentimes, it is a reflection upon them and where they currently are, not upon you. Don't let that sort of thing prevent you from achieving your goals. But don't revel in your successes and rub other people's noses in it either. That's one of the things that I suppose I did wrong (though I thought he would be happy for me). It almost caused another situation…ironically also at Karaoke Night, but in a different place and an earlier time.

When I was actively seeking out girls, I used online dating as a way to get more leverage. I knew that being a strongman would help improve my "marketability" so I had put it into my online profile.

One of the girls who had messaged me said that her ideal first date was karaoke. Well, I enjoy karaoke as well (as you should know by now) and looked for places, but didn't find any. So we settled on meeting at the bar for drinks.

I arrived at the bar, met her and the attraction just wasn't there. Oh well, at least we could chat and have fun talking and keeping each other company.

As we sat down for drinks she asked me a lot of questions about being a strongman. She had a lot of theater background, so was fascinated by me being a strongman since she was unfamiliar with it.

As we were talking, I noticed that they were setting up a sound system in the back of the bar.

"Hey what are they doing?" I asked the bartender.

"We are setting up for our first karaoke night here," she said.

My date and I both looked at each other with the same expression, "Great!"

My date went first and had an amazing voice that was built through years of theater and choir. Everyone was impressed. It was my turn and I sang a song by the Scorpions. I was okay, I guess.

During the date I left my drink with my date and went to the bathroom. When I came back out there was a guy talking to my date and blocking my beer.

"Excuse me sir, you seem to be blocking my beer," I said politely. He was a good five inches taller than me…and obviously interested in the date that I wasn't really attracted to from the get go.

"You suck at singing," He said to me trying to make me look bad in front of my date. Some people push others down to try to make themselves look better, rather than go on their own merits. It usually defeats the purpose because they themselves appear bitter and jealous. On top of that, telling someone they suck at singing no matter how bad they are is a breach of karaoke etiquette. My date knew this and whatever chance he might have had with her he just blew.

"Oh really? I haven't seen you up there, are you going to show me how it's done?" I say back to him.

"I also suck at singing," he says.

"Well maybe you ought not to try to push people down for having the courage to go up in front of people," I say to him. "And you are still blocking my beer."

"This is my bar," he said ballooning his chest. Is this guy kidding me? It was like something out of a cheesy eighties movie. My date, who knew that I was a strongman, was entertained by this exchange. I could see it out of the corner of my eye.

I considered saying, "Do you want to know what I do with bars?" and show him my video but I figured that would probably push this guy over the edge because he's obviously insecure. Then we'd have a situation like with Dan.

Instead I said, "This is your bar? Nice place you got here. But nevertheless I'm a paying customer and you are still blocking my beer." and with that I pulled my chair out slightly pushing him out of the way with it and sat in it with my back to him.

I knew that there were two ways this situation would go. He would either hit me in the back of the head or he would walk away with his tail between his legs. I gambled that he would do the latter.

Had I told him about the whole strongman thing he likely wouldn't have believed me and brought about a situation like the one previously mentioned.

Had he actually been nice about the whole thing and if my date was interested, I might have respectfully bowed out.

Being nice will get you a lot farther than trying to push people down.

CONEY ISLAND: THE PLAYGROUND OF THE WORLD, THE STOMPING GROUND OF THE STRONGMEN.

"Yeah, I'll take you to Coney Island to see the strongman spectacular. Greg will be there," I said acting as if I was relenting. The truth was I wanted to go and I wanted someone to be there with me and she was the closest thing I had to a girlfriend at that point.

"Yay!" Sarah said, raising one shoulder as she said it. "I'm so excited!" Sarah was a horseback riding instructor who I had recently started dating. She was originally from Rhode Island but had relocated here to New Jersey to manage a barn. She was blond-haired blue-eyed and petite with impeccable posture from being upright on horses for the better part of her adult life.

She had a particular fondness for Coca Cola, the *Dukes of Hazard* and country music. We seemed to be opposites in a sense that she was a little bit of country and I was a little bit of heavy metal, but we got along great.

Even though we didn't have a label on it, we were practically boyfriend and girlfriend at that point. I hadn't gone on a date with another girl for about two weeks, but I was still hesitant to jump into something when there were a lot of girls interested in me on Match.com. She was the first one though and I liked her, but I wasn't ready to be exclusive yet. I was hesitant to jump into a relationship since I had been exclusive for a decade and got burned because of it and I was enjoying being an eligible bachelor.

The Coney Island Strongman Spectacular marked a big occasion. The previous year was the first time in six decades that the strongmen had been there. This had been the stomping ground for the Mighty Atom and many of the top guys would be there. It was a big step forward for the return of the strongmen and I was an up and comer. Maybe one day I'll be on the Coney Island stage. Greg was grooming me to be able to do that at some point, but I still had a lot of work to do. As a strongman, I can always get a bit stronger and I will strive to do so.

We drove down; I found a place to park and called Greg to figure out where I was going. We found the place at the boardwalk and there was a roped off area for the people who had purchased tickets while others could sit outside that area.

It was a beautiful summer day, the weather was perfect for the outdoor strongman show and I led Sarah around by the hand while I looked around for food, a bathroom (it had been a long drive after all) and also for some of the familiar faces I hadn't seen yet.

I found another student of Greg's, named Bill Solony, and his daughter and asked where Greg was. He was behind the stage, this time he had a cane…and he didn't have his new dog. That was odd because he would go everywhere with his dog.

He looked like he was in more pain than usual.

"Hey Greg, this is Sarah, the girl I've been seeing."

Greg was stoic for as long as I had known him and has a monotone way of speaking, but I could tell that he was in more pain that day than he normally was. The fact that he was walking around with a cane was indicative of that.

"Very nice to meet you," Greg said extending his hand. I had told him about her so now he could put a face to the name.

Sarah had known about Greg, too. Greg was the subject of many of my conversations with her about the power that we have within ourselves. That was the subject of the lessons Greg was giving me.

The Coney Island Strongman show started. It was an outdoor event and it was the perfect weather for it. Adam Rinn was the emcee of the event that day and many of the strongmen who are active today were showcased here. Chris Rider (who would later coach me) set a world record that day and even the legendary Slim the Hammer Man performed using a crusher (an old exercise tool that people from the audience attempted to use and couldn't).

Slim had a couple people try to close the ends together and when they couldn't do it proving the difficulty of the feat, Slim took the thing and brought the ends together over eighty times before it broke. How many could he have done? Who knows? One thing is for sure though, at the time, he was in his upper seventies and able to do things even the young guys can't. That is one of the many things that make him legendary.

Before he had done that though, another strongman named The Mighty Stefan had challenged me on the sidelines to go up and close it.

I introduced myself and said back to him, "I'm actually an up and coming strongman being trained by Greg…I'm pretty sure I can close it."

It wouldn't have looked good for the show if I went and closed it and Stefan knew that, so he smiled and nodded, understanding that I was probably not the best one to choose.

The Mighty Stefan was a student of Mike Greenstein. Mike Greenstein was the son of the Mighty Atom, so he was one of the true torchbearers of old-time strongmanism. He is the strongman who is oftentimes chosen to be the emcee at the AOBS dinner. He's got a great way with words and some of the stories I've heard from him sound like they could be from the most interesting man character that you see in Dos Equis commercials.

Stefan saw that I had brought some steel with me and I told him what I had planned on doing with it. He smiled his approval.

"Very nice to meet you young man," he said smiling through his beard. I had seen him at the strongman dinner plenty of times, but never as a strongman, and I hadn't introduced myself to him yet at that point.

Sarah and I watched the Coney Island Strongman Spectacular from the sidelines as we admired each strongman display his unique feats. Each one got a different reaction from the crowd. Each feat showed that impossible is simply a state of mind.

I hear the emcee say, "And the star of Bending Steel…Chris 'Wonder' Schoeck!"

I stand there watching this with particular interest because Chris is my size. If he's capable of it, so am I. And one day that will be me on the stage, bending steel in Coney Island.

When it was all said and done and the crowd started to disperse I sought out Slim because I wanted to do something special. I was going to bend the steel bar on my nose for a legend, in Coney Island...one of the stomping grounds of the Mighty Atom, his mentor. The very first person who I had heard did this was Slim and this was my way of paying homage to a legend.

After that Slim joked with Sarah, "I'd like to take you home, but I'm old and not sure I'd remember what to do with you." She looked back, being entertained. Slim...always charming the ladies.

We walked around trying to find Greg but he was nowhere to be found. The following week I went to Greg's to continue my strongman training and found out why he left early.

Turns out it was because it was too painful for him to stand. New Jersey's Superman needed medical help. Nobody should be in so much pain. Greg was mentally strong and this would have brought a lesser man to his knees a lot sooner.

His dog wasn't with him because the new one was not the dog that Greg thought he would be. The dog was vicious and not capable of being a pet. My memory is fuzzy on this, but I think it had attacked Greg.

Later that week, while Sarah was back at the ranch where she worked and lived, I went to the studio where I was training people that morning when I got a text from Sarah.

"I just called the police on Grace. She just tried to strangle me. I need you to come get me. Can I stay with you?"

I looked at the text in shock. I had given Sarah a recorder to record their conversations, I knew she was being mentally abused and things were bad between her and her boss/landlord Grace, but this was whole a new level entirely.

She couldn't stay in a hotel because Grace had refused to pay her even though she had done the work, which is not legal, but it would take time to get the money for which she worked.

Things needed to be changed and changed now...and yet this girl who I had only been seeing a couple weeks was going to be living with me in my house.

Now I was on high alert because it was too soon for this sort of thing. But what could I do? I couldn't just abandon her or leave her in a dangerous situation. She had nowhere else to go. I consider myself to be a good guy so the choice was obvious.

"Yeah I'll come get you, and yes, you can stay with me," I texted back to her. "Are you safe?"

"Yes, the police are here."

Okay good. I left and got her as soon as I could.

The police had left, so I scanned the ranch looking for danger. Grace and her husband had left, too. Maybe in handcuffs...I never asked. I only was concerned whether or not Sarah was okay.

I arrived on the ranch with adrenaline in my veins, scanning for any possible signs of danger. If danger showed, I was ready. I had no idea if Grace and her husband had come back and were going to try something or not. The only thing I knew was that I wasn't going to let it happen. We packed up her belongings, which wasn't a lot, considering she had lived there for a while and we headed to my house.

When we got to my house I got some of her stuff and saw her at the top of the stairs, crying about the whole thing. Scared, outcast, away from her real home in Rhode Island, feeling like she was imposing on me and with the after effects of a horrible day and the uncertainty of things to come.

She was out of a job, had no money and no place to stay except with a guy she had only been seeing a couple weeks.

I didn't know what else to say to make her comfortable other than looking her in the eyes and saying, "You're safe here."

But nevertheless, she had moved in. We didn't have any other options after all. She got on the phone with her father to tell him everything that had transpired.

"I'm staying with my boyfriend," She reassured him. I guess I'm her boyfriend. She was living here after all. I'm not exactly going to go on any other dates while she's living here.

"Thank you for letting my daughter stay with you," her father said to me over the phone.

I knew she told him about me, but this man had yet to meet me. I'm sure he was nervous for the safety of his daughter so I tried to appear as honorable and respectful as possible.

"You're welcome, sir," I said.

I knew though, as much as I liked her, this relationship wouldn't last. It was too soon for her to move in and she needed to get her life together and the only way to do that was for her to move back home with her family.

I got on the phone with Greg and gave him the rundown of what had happened and told him I was going to put my strongman training on hold, just for a little bit, to spend the limited time I had left with her.

Now while Sarah was staying with me, she noticed one day while I was checking my email that my eyes bugged out of my head, giddy with excitement.

"What's up?" she asked me.

There is a personal training certification workshop in Minnesota and I was being invited. There was just one problem, it was the same weekend of the Association of Oldetime Barbell and Strongman dinner where I had met Greg and I knew he would want me to be on stage.

I figured the workshop was probably going to be bigger for my career as a personal trainer; that was the choice that I made and I sent in my application. I didn't tell Greg because I was afraid of disappointing him.

Sarah and I enjoyed what time we could with each other before she had to go. She was interested in maintaining a long distance relationship, but I knew it wouldn't work no matter how strongly I was starting to feel.

The final day came and she woke up earlier than me. She sat there watching me sleep, crying. I woke up and looked at her.

"You couldn't be a jerk, you had to be amazing," she said between her teardrops.

I held her and told her that she had made me the happiest I've felt in a long time, thanking her as my eyes welled up. My first bit of real companionship since my divorce.

I went to walk her to her car and wanted to leave a parting gift with her. I took a steel bar and bent it on the bridge of my nose for her to remember me by. She took it with tears in her eyes. Tears were in my eyes too as she looked at me saying, "You know I'm coming back for you, right?" I nodded yes, even though I knew it wasn't true.

I spent the rest of the weekend in bed with a broken heart staring at the ceiling fan. What would be the point of getting out of bed when you are feeling this sad? No, I had a purpose and that purpose would resume again the following weekend.

I went back to Greg's on a beautiful summer's day.

"She's gone Greg," I said. At this point, Greg was more than just a guide. He was a close friend that I had the privilege of knowing, learning from and just spending time with.

I showed him the footage that Sarah had taken of me bending the steel bar on my nose for her (to this date that's the shortest one I've done). I told him it was my parting gift to her as he treated me to a frosty beverage from the local 7-11 to pick up my spirits. I'm thankful to be able to give something like that and I'm thankful to Greg for helping me find my own strength.

"I'm very proud of you," he said reviewing the footage. "You've come a long way."

"When do you think I'll be ready to be a professional old-time performing strongman?"

"I think you're ready now. You just need to find someone to pay you to be a professional."

I'm ready now? Wow! I felt newly invigorated at this turn of events.

"You're ready now, but I'd like to make you into a better strongman than I ever was. With your dedication and learning from my success and mistakes, it could happen."

"I don't know Greg, I've seen some of the stuff you did, and it's a pretty tall order. I want to be as great as I can possibly be though. I'm all in."

"I'll help you. I consider you more than a student. You're a friend now. I'd like to spend some time on the beach with Karen this summer. We can pick back up in the fall."

"You're a good friend as well, Greg." I myself was looking forward to some beach days, some of them with different girls, none of whom would amount to anything, but I would spend many of them on my own staring contemplatively at the water.

I love beach days. Something about the ocean makes me feel very content. You give me ocean and sand and I am happy as a clam.

Greg and I had agreed that my mentoring by one of the best strongman coaches in the world, a good man and a good friend would resume in the fall. It never did.

I would become his *last student*.

THE LAST SON OF KRYPTON

The summer came and went. I practiced the old-time feats of strength on my own, bending various things and looked forward to resuming my strongman training in the fall. I was very busy, trying to run a personal training business, coordinating meetup groups, going out on dates and I also had a fundraiser I was trying to promote for St. Jude's Children's Research Hospital. My publicist and I were going back and forth with the newspapers and press releases and a whole bunch of other stuff.

The St Jude's fundraiser is something I do to celebrate my birthday by doing what I love. Coaching people, doing old-time feats of strength and raising money for sick kids so that they can have more birthdays. With everything going on, my mentorship with Greg would have to be put on the back burner for just a little bit longer.

We had put it in the newspapers that if I raised the goal money, I would bend a steel bar on the bridge of my nose. I chose that because it was Greg's favorite feat, was becoming a specialty of mine since it's rare and I wanted people to pony up the cash. I wanted to raise money for those kids pretty badly. Everything else would simply have to wait.

The day of the St. Jude's fundraiser came and we had a reporter there to report on the event. The goal money was raised so steel was going to get bent on the bridge of my nose. The newspaper reporter was fascinated with it.

"How on earth do you do that?" she asked.

"It's the power of the mind over the body," I replied going into a short explanation so that she could get it into the paper.

"How did you discover that you could do this?"

"I have a mentor down in South Jersey who guided me and helped me discover the power that we all have within. Without him, I may never have discovered that I can do this," I told her truthfully.

I remembered having a conversation with Greg where he wanted me to say I graduated some school and I wanted to tell the papers I was mentored. Kind of like the Karate Kid or Rocky.

Two weeks later, I was in the Newark airport heading out to Minnesota for the personal training certification workshop. I had on my effects that represent that I'm a strongman, including the shirt Greg gave me the first time I bent a steel bar on my nose in his gym.

It was the same weekend as the Association of Oldetime Barbell and Strongman Dinner where I had met Greg and it would take place the following day less than a half-mile from where I was at that moment.

I sat there on the plane looking at the other flights flying in, as we were getting ready to fly out. I wondered how many strongmen were going to be flying in that day while I was on my way out.

I felt a sense of guilt about not going to the dinner as Greg's student and I felt something was wrong. I didn't know what it was…just something felt wrong.

I got to Minnesota without too much of a fuss and found Tony, the person I would be sharing a room with later that evening by talking with another trainer that I had previously met.

I sat down with them and had a spirited conversation about my new venture as a strongman. I showed them the video Greg had taken of me bending a steel bar with my nose in his gym and they loved it. It was something I had talked about with a great deal of pride and I was not shy about telling them whom I was learning from. I was proud to be the student of New Jersey's Superman himself. It made me feel…cool.

The next morning the certification workshop had started and we were going through some of the progressions and there was a questions and answers section. I volunteered a question though I don't remember what it was. I remember the answer though.

"Get stronger," Pavel said while smiling. Everyone laughed including myself.

He then explained the joke.

"Ladies and gentlemen, I kid with Eric, of course. I know that he's very strong having seen video of him doing fifty consecutive one legged squats and I know he's a strongman who rolls up frying pans and bends steel bars."

I smiled at this. Pavel was a subject matter expert on strength to the Marine's, Navy Seals and other groups where strength can't be faked. His books were one of the things that put the bug of strength into me and led me to Dave Whitley, who led me to my mentor Greg Matonick.

After Pavel had given his explanation, a hush fell over the other candidates as they now were viewing me differently. I fielded questions during one of the breaks as I got my second or third cup of coffee holding it up and jokingly saying, "This is the source of my power." I figured since we were on break, maybe now would be a good time to check my messages.

There was a text from Dave Whitley, my first strongman friend, who had first introduced me to Greg. Greg was the one who showed me the true source of my power was inside me this whole time.

"Greg passed away yesterday morning," It said.

I stared at the text in shock and did a double take…What? This can't be true, how can this be true? What the hell happened?

I called him and it was the phone call that he knew would come and the one he was dreading all day.

"Hey brother," He said solemnly. Nobody likes to be the bearer of bad news and this was about as bad as they come.

"Iron Tamer…What happened? What the hell happened???"

"It was complications from his back surgery. I'm sorry brother."

For some reason I didn't cry.

Instead, I felt as if I was the one who died. I lost all feeling. I was floating around like I was a ghost and went back to the workshop, but was unable to concentrate on anything. I was lost, without a mentor and without my friend. The strongman who put the broken man back on his feet was gone.

Later that evening, I was in the hotel and Tony, my roommate, found me sitting on the bed staring at a television that wasn't even on. A look of concern crossed his eyebrows.

"You okay, man?"

"No."

"What happened?"

"My strongman mentor passed away."

He stood there stunned.

"How?"

"Complications from a surgery he had."

"I'm sorry man. I can't even imagine."

Tony was a black belt in Brazilian Jujitsu and we had a mutual respect though we had just met in person the night before. He knew the value that a good teacher can provide, not just in technique, but adding value to someone's life and knew that no words that he could say would make this any better.

"I'm going to head to the bar downstairs and have some drinks with some of the guys. You should come with me. It might help get your mind off of things," He offered.

I nodded.

"I need to shower."

When I went downstairs some of the guys down there that knew me from

Internet forums or had met me gave their condolences.

I felt a tremendous responsibility to make sure the world knew what Greg did for me and that it was up to me to keep *strongmanism* alive in his absence.

I was the last student of New Jersey's Superman - Greg Matonick. My memory gets a bit fuzzy at this point, but I believe it was during the following conversations that someone dubbed me "The Last Son of Krypton." It was done as a tribute to him, not to cash in on the popularity of Superman the comic book, movie, toys and cartoon franchise.

I only remember the first parts of the evening. The rest of it I have no recollection of. I don't know how I got back to my room. I don't know whom I talked to. It isn't like me to not remember the things I do.

I would find out about a year and a half later that I had a two and a half hour long conversation, that I have no recollection of, with a guy I couldn't remember named Jody Beasly. He told me that I spoke about how it was my responsibility to keep *strongmanism* alive and to make Greg live on through my feats.

After my flight home I walked up my stairs and saw the very first *scrollpture* I had ever done sitting on my coffee table and lost control of my tears. I looked around my house and the same thing would happen time and time again.

All of those empty picture hooks that were up around my house, the empty hooks that previously had pictures of my ex-wife and me, that had stood empty as a painful reminder of a life I wished to leave behind, now had some of the steel that I had bent up there.

The first pretzel scroll I ever did… The piece of twenty-four inch reinforcing bar I had done which gave me the idea for Rebar to Ribbons. The first steel bar I ever bent on my nose, which would become a bit of a signature bend.

Those pieces now occupied the empty hooks, a reminder of the journey I was on. The strongman's journey. And the one who made it all possible I would never see again.

I never asked him to sign my Mighty Atom book though I had many opportunities. I never had my picture taken with him though I had my camera with me every time I was with him. Now it was too late. I couldn't get any of those things with the man who changed everything. You just never know.

When it came time to go to the funeral, I was unsure of what to wear. Normally you wear a black suit but I had to wear something symbolic of my time with him. Would I be out of place if I wore my strongman shirt? I opted to do that, to represent what he had done.

I took the steel bar I had bent on my nose for St. Jude's with me to give to Karen, Greg's widow. I had wanted to give it to Greg and wouldn't have the opportunity but she could have it in his place. I wanted her to know that I wasn't going to waste what he had taught me. I was going to do great things for the world with it. St. Jude's would be symbolic of that. I also brought a letter for her that I wrote when I finally had a chance to collect my thoughts.

I neared the funeral parlor and it was packed. Found myself a parking space and tried to relax the knot in my stomach as I walked into the strongest funeral I ever went to.

There were strongmen everywhere because he had touched so many people not just by teaching the ones who wished to learn, but because he was a generous man. He was the all-around strongman that he wished to impart on me.

Inside were commonplace things you would typically see in a funeral. Pictures of loved ones and family members and fond memories decorated the various tables and easels. Things that were uniquely Greg also decorated the area. Greg liked switchblades; I had vivid recollections of him eating fruit using one as a utensil. There were things representative of Frankenstein because that was Greg's favorite monster (because he was the strongest). I think Frankenstein had resonated with Greg on a different level besides strength also.

There was a video booth where you could sit in and say a few things about him. I opted to say a few words. I'm going to paraphrase what I said, but the key points are still the same.

"Greg came along during the hardest period of my life, to teach me things about myself and to pull me back on my feet when I had prayed to God for strength. I think he may have been the angel sent to be my guiding light."

Angels aren't always what you expect. Sometimes they come looking like they belong in a motorcycle gang, covered in tattoos. It is what they do and how they help that makes them real life angels.

His daughter, Kira, delivered the Eulogy, talking about some of Greg's struggles, his generosity, his fondness for strength and the Mighty Atom book, his love of Jesus and him as a father. It was hard for me to say good-bye; I can only imagine what it was like for his wife and daughter.

When I came around to say good-bye to the ashes of my mentor and friend I simply said, "Thank you Greg, I'm going to miss you. I promise to keep you alive through the feats of strength that you taught me."

After the funeral we headed back to Greg's gym where I had been through so many breakthroughs under his generosity and mentorship.

It was a bit surreal. Greg had taught me so many lessons using some of the other strongmen as examples and here they were, walking around in his gym, but without him here. Not in the physical sense anyways.

In this gym, Greg's gym, so many breakthroughs had taken place. Not just with me but with the other strongmen who had passed through over the years. I wasn't the first. I was simply the last.

As the other strongmen had taken some of the various things to remember him by, I opted to take the Zass scroll as a remembrance. It was a piece of steel, bent by New Jersey's Superman himself with his writing on it. He may not have signed my Atom book, but I at least had something tangible.

The Zass scroll was something that he had wanted to teach to me but we never got around to it. At least I could use this to try to reverse engineer it. In a sense he did teach it to me.

I handed the letter to Karen along with a newspaper clipping from the St. Jude's Fundraiser and the steel bar I had bent on my nose, the feat he taught me I used to raise the goal money for sick kids. I wanted her to know that the time he spent with me on the last year of his life was going to be for a good cause. I was not going to waste it. He started me on the path and pointed me in the direction to go. I just had to walk it, alone.

I wasn't alone though. Greg would always be there in the lessons he taught and he had prepared me well. Now it's my turn to use what he had taught me.

I need to do a show. An honorable show, so he can watch me from heaven. What he taught me must not be lost.

MY FIRST BOOKED SHOW AND BUD JEFFRIES

I had heard a story about a fundraiser for a local girl who was diagnosed with cancer and had no medical insurance to help pay for it. Some of the fundraiser volunteers were looking for local business' to donate some gift baskets to enter into a tricky tray auction.

When things like this come along, sometimes I would offer vouchers that would be good towards my personal training services because I like giving back to the community. Yeah, I might not make any money from it but hopefully I get a bit of good Karma and it makes me feel good anyway.

The spot where this particular fundraiser was being held was an hour or so from my training studio so it was highly unlikely anybody there would be interested and I was trying to get on my feet as a strongman anyways. Now was my opportunity to get my feet wet with a good cause and honor Greg by doing a good deed using the things he taught me.

"Hey Patty, I would be honored to donate my services as an entertainer," I said. "I'll perform legitimate old-time feats of strength and give a nice message about the power of the human spirit. If there are any kids there, they'll love it."

"Thank you so much," she said. "I'll pass your info along to the organizers."

A couple days later I'm driving along in my car on the way back from my training studio and I get a call on my cell phone.

"Hi, I got your number from Patty. I understand you were interested in donating your services to our fundraiser," the woman on the phone said.

"Yes, I'd be honored to."

The woman on the end of the line was a close friend of the fundraiser recipient. She said the woman who was sick was the kind of person who was always thinking of others and would give you the shirt off of her back if you needed it. When she was diagnosed with cancer she had no medical insurance to cover it so her friends decided to organize a fundraiser to help out. She sounded like an amazing person and I like amazing people so it's an honor for me to do what I do and spread the message of internal strength.

"Great! You know it means a lot that everybody is helping out. I'm going to put you in the schedule for that date," she said.

I was just booked in advanced for the very first time. This was a stepping stone as I got closer to being a legitimate professional performing strongman and it was going to be a great experience.

As the day got closer I practiced my lines, put together the soundtrack and figured out the show. I didn't add the nose bend to the list because I wasn't completely sure how kids would react to that one. I know some of the adults I've done it in front of wince and sometimes even get a bit queasy. People can sometimes have strange reactions upon seeing things they perceive as impossible. After all, steel bars aren't supposed to be bent by human beings and especially not on the bridge of their nose.

I had recently begun a relationship with my current girlfriend, Diara, and she once told me that's her favorite feat that I do. I think her favorite feat that I do now is turning a horseshoe into a heart. At the time though it was bending steel on my nose.

Diara is a petite Italian girl with a fondness of Malbec wines and dark chocolate. We met in the aftermath of hurricane Sandy and the sheer beauty of her eyes hypnotized me. Thankfully she seemed into me too. She said that the whole idea of me being a strongman was "intriguing" so when I asked to be exclusive, I did it right after bending a thick steel bar for her.

Anyways, I paced up and down the hallway of my home while Diara put on her make-up and straightened her hair. To me she looked beautiful no matter what, but she is especially beautiful when she puts herself together. I oftentimes watch her getting ready, putting a lot of care and thought into her appearance and I think to myself "Surely there has to be a faster way."

There isn't to the best of my knowledge and I was especially impatient that day...the day of my first stand alone show.

I paced up and down the hallway; I checked the steel, the frying pans and other things I decided to wreck in the name of goodwill, time and time again while I waited. Ugh, I wished I was just there already.

We headed on over and I introduced myself to everyone there and handed my soundtrack to the DJ. He'd never heard of what I do. That's all fine and good because it needs to be experienced anyways.

It was my time to shine.

"Good afternoon everybody," I proceeded to ramble on something about the human spirit and the superhero in all of us.

I moved on to do some of the feats; I bent a thick steel bar and handed it to one of the kids who was delighted to get it. I went for the pretzel scroll but I must have miss-measured it because I was unable to get the second loop across. I held it up and said, "A goose!" to attempt to recover and I rolled up three frying pans and gave another message of the power of the human spirit as my voice quivered. I wouldn't see how much till afterwards.

Greg, I'll get better I promise.

I got applause and everybody loved the show. I felt like a big shot, but looking back at it now, I had a lot of work to do if I was going to be big. I'd come to realize this when I saw a strongman named Bud Jeffries later that week.

I had first read about Bud Jeffries in a book written by Pavel Tsatsouline named *Beyond Bodybuilding*. Bud was a full time performing strongman who had once dead squatted nine-hundred pounds, swung a fifty-three pound kettlebell for two thousand four hundred fifty consecutive repetitions and was capable of things that human beings of this Earth shouldn't be capable of.

I hadn't realized it at the time but he was the one who introduced Dave Whitley to Dennis Rogers who would mentor him and bring him into the strongman world. Dave Whitley would become the Iron Tamer and later on introduce me to Greg Matonick who would do the same for me. With Bud's accomplishments and also because he was someone I read about time and time again; he was like a superhero come to life. I was thrilled when he called me up to invite me to see a school assembly he was doing in my area.

I had gotten caught in early morning traffic, so I arrived a little bit late to his school assembly but luckily I only missed one feat. I witnessed the hold he had on these youngsters as he went through his routine. He was polished, professional, entertaining and he had the absolute attention of the impressionable young minds he was in front of. He was telling them messages that I believe people both young and old need to hear. Things like believe in yourself and be good to others. The feats were the side dish that connected the dots. They weren't the main course.

It was time for the finale feat and Bud Jeffries announced to the audience, "I have a friend here I'd like to introduce. His name is Eric Moss and he's also a strongman."

I walked up, smiled and waved to everybody. I was sharing the stage with Bud Jeffries. This was awesome but nerve-wracking at the same time. Awesome because he was a true professional, a legend in the making, and it gave me a chance to see the potential for changing lives using our own unique skill set.

Nerve-wracking because after seeing Bud perform I realized that this was the high bar I have to reach to be a top dog and also because of the inherent danger of the finale feat itself.

I was to drop a bowling ball onto Bud's stomach from the top of the ladder.

What if I mess this up?

What if I drop it on the wrong spot?

The spot where it's intended to hit is just inches away from his sternum and inches away from his groin. The forces involved with this are high which is why the feat is saved for the finale.

He put a dinner plate onto his stomach to use as a target as I climbed up and looked down at him from a top the ladder and held the bowling ball over him. He gestured where to move the bowling ball so it would land in the right spot and the countdown began.

"10." Ten seconds left.

"9." Nine seconds left.

"8." Eight seconds left.

"7." Seven seconds left.

"6." Six seconds left.

"5." Only five seconds left.

"4." The anticipation builds.

"3." Not much time left now.

"2." I hope I don't mess this up.

"1." Well there's no turning back now, here goes nothing.

I could feel the weight of it at the ends of my outstretched arms as I attempted to let go of both sides at the exact same time hoping it didn't shift to his sternum or groin. I watched the bowling ball descend in slow motion inching its way closer to the target.

CRASH! I heard the plate shatter and the bowling ball drop to the floor as I watched him to make sure he was okay.

He made a sound joking like I killed him while the children screamed in amazement and glee at what they just saw. I let out a sigh of relief as he gave me the thumbs up that he was fine. Whew! So glad I didn't hurt him.

I climbed down the ladder as he gave his final words of advice and we both bowed and waved to the kids at the end of the show. The teachers and administrative staff at this school came over to tell him how much they loved the show and thanked both of us. No need to thank me because I was happy to be able to be a part of it and to learn from him by watching how he did things. It pays to model success especially if you are unsure about how to do things.

Bud and I headed out to get a cup of coffee so I could pick his brain and learn from someone who has walked the path I wish to walk. I sipped my coffee while he critiqued video footage of the show I had done the week prior. I had just witnessed a rock star performance and we were now looking at a tape of a garage band...my garage band. It was good because it's important not to kid myself into thinking I didn't need any work. Work has to be had if I was going to be successful in this business.

"You see here this one kid is looking around," He said pointing to one of the audience members. "It's because they are unsure of what they are supposed to be doing. You need to connect the audience to the feats otherwise you're just a person grunting in the front of the room," He said. I sort of knew this already but I needed to take it to a new level now that I saw what the level actually was.

Listening to him talk about putting together shows, connecting to the audience and using it to change lives was priceless advice but only if I acted upon it. Acting upon it, would help me change lives. It was only a matter of time and work.

"I'll get there," I thought to myself. "I know I will. I must."

It's only a matter of time and work.

TRICKS FOR BREADSTICKS

I knew how rare *strongmanism* was because I didn't even know such a thing existed 'til I was in my mid to late twenties. I was fascinated by it, by what the old-timers did to build incredible levels of strength before steroids existed and also what the few modern day guys were doing.

When you hear the word "strongman," people are usually using it to describe competition strongmen. When I would try to describe being a strongman, I oftentimes would compare it to a magician, so that they could grasp that it was a form of entertainment.

I would say things like, "Picture a magic show. ' As you can see the hat is empty'" referring to the rabbit in the hat trick which just about everybody has seen before. It's something they are familiar with and the trick with teaching is connecting something by relating something unfamiliar to something familiar.

"Now replace the illusions with old-time feats of strength like bending steel bars, ripping open horseshoes, rolling up frying pans, bending spikes and that sort of thing," I would say.

I had also kept a promotional video on my phone that I would use to explain what I was doing, and I had also used it as a way to impress girls. I had sent the video online to my girlfriend Diara while we were still talking online before we had met in person to try and impress her. I bent a steel bar on my leg right before I asked her to go steady, too. That was because it was the best way I could think of to be romantic at that moment in time...but that's a different story, the details of which are between myself and Diara...and maybe the friends she gossips the juicy stuff to.

Anyways, knowing the format was similar to magic and knowing that everybody knows what a magician is, I started looking around at local magicians to see who was established and who I might be able ride the coattails of and pick their brain from an entertainment standpoint (there's more to doing a good show then simply doing the thing. Like Bud Jeffries had told me, they need to connect to the feats). As I searched on Google and some of the websites entertainers use to promote themselves, one name kept popping up. Marco.

Marco was a magician who was based in the town where I grew up so there was a familiarity there. I hadn't seen him in action, but I had seen that he appeared in a music video and was doing a lot of shows. This was a man who knows what's up.

I looked up his Facebook page awaiting the right time to reach out. Unfortunately, the right time to reach out would be birthed out of a tragedy.

The Sandy Hook massacre.

After the Sandy Hook massacre, Marco wanted to put on a show for the kids free of charge to lift their spirits. He reached out on Facebook to see if any magicians would be interested in doing a free show. Just like the last fundraiser, I couldn't turn down this opportunity to do something great for the kids following that horrific event.

I commented on his post, "I'm not a magician, I'm an old-time performing strongman and I would be honored to be a part of it." I enjoy doing things for goodwill; it's what Greg called being the all-around strongman.

Following that, Marco asked to meet me in a local diner we were both familiar with to discuss what I do. I told him I had the singular goal of getting paid for a show so that I could be a legitimate professional and do right by my mentor.

"I'm very impressed by you my friend. I'll be able to get you a paid gig. It will happen, it's only a matter of time and work," he told me.

Sometime later one of Marco's magician friends, Joe, was doing a fundraiser for the hungry. Marco would have been on the bill, but there was a scheduling conflict for him, so knowing what I do he recommended me. I was happy to do it because even though I wasn't going to be paid it was still a step forward. This would be the first time I would have a fully contained show, on stage, announced ahead of time and everything. It also was the first time I would appear with world-renowned magicians.

Now appearing on the same bill as a magician can be risky for someone who does what I do. What magicians do is an illusion. What I do are authentic feats of strength. I love magic and watch it whenever I get the opportunity but it's a very different beast and it's very important to my craft to make sure that I am not deceptive in any way, shape or form.

I know some of the strongmen who are out there won't appear with magicians because they think people will believe them to be fake. Guilt by association. I think the opposite.

As long as people are told ahead of time that it's different, they completely understand. I know it has helped me out a lot. When we can all respect the hats we each individually wear, all will prosper in the end.

Marco tells me that Joe is a good guy and someone I should definitely meet. Joe and his wife have a lot of experience and oftentimes like to help out the up and comers in the magic world. They even created their own stage for doing so. I meet with Joe and his wife ahead of time to talk about the specifics of the show and what I would need.

I needed a bowl of M&Ms in the dressing room with all of the brown ones removed otherwise I'm not doing the show. I kid, of course (Van Halen rocks)! I'm no prima donna.

I tried to keep things simple. Give me something to play my music through, something to amplify my voice, an audience ready to witness the power and I'll do the rest. Nowadays, sometimes I use a projector and have my own screen, microphone and everything. I'm mostly self-contained. It really depends on the show and the needs of the client.

At that time, before I added more speaking and developed my motivational speaking skills, my show was about fifteen minutes long. Fifteen minutes with an introduction to the different feats. Since this was a magic show, I planned on bringing people up to the stage to authenticate the different feats. When it came time for the triple frying pan roll up, I would have the volunteer reveal what was in each of the bags. I hadn't realized when I planned this that I would have some special volunteers.

Diara's sister is a talented photographer and she was going to take pictures of the event. Her boyfriend and mother were going to come, too. My mom and dad were also going to come, so this was going to be the first time that they would meet. Now the pressure was on. Oh boy, I hoped this would go well.

The day comes and Diara and I drive down there a bit ahead of time. She didn't particularly care for the way I was dressed and made sure to let me know about it, but I knew that there can be a lot of pressure put on my clothes, so I wasn't going to dress any differently than when I practice. I do dress a bit nicer now that I've found jeans of the right material and give freedom of movement, but at the time I was still figuring things out for myself.

So we arrived there and I went backstage before the people started coming in for the show. A world-renowned magician named Al Callus was on before me and I could hear what he was doing but couldn't really see it. I would have liked to have seen his act, but the more important thing was to make sure I was in the right frame of mind for my show.

The emcee for the event gave me a pre-introduction making sure the audience knew that what I was doing wasn't magic. It was coming to that special time. Time for me to do my thing and let the things that Greg taught me take over.

I walked out from behind the curtain and started shaking out my muscles getting them ready for action. I had paid a guy who does the voice over for movie trailers to give me an introduction over top of the music I had. All of a sudden the curtains went up, about a minute ahead of time and I was on the stage with everybody looking at me. I thought to myself "Oh crap. What do I do?"

I struck a pose and tried my best to look majestic and statuesque 'til it was my turn to talk. I folded my arms across my chest trying to look like a tough guy and awaited my cue,

"...and now...Eric Moss."

"Good evening, everybody. My name is Eric Moss and I'm an old-time performing strongman. Old-time *strongmanism* and strength exhibitionism is an old and nearly forgotten form of entertainment that predates Vaudeville and remained popular in music halls and carnivals. It remained alive only by the few teachers who knew the techniques and would teach them to those they deemed strong and worthy enough. I was mentored by New Jersey's Superman - the late Greg Matonick - and I was the last student he had before he passed away which is how I got the name the Last Son of Krypton. What he taught me and what I'm going to perform for you today are legitimate old-time feats of strength. I promise you nothing has been tampered with. Everything you are going to see is real. Is everybody ready?" I said out loud to the darkness.

With the spotlight on me it was difficult to make out the various faces in the audience, but I knew they were there.

"For the first feat, I'll need a volunteer."

I saw some raised hands and picked out one of them and they stood up to come to the stage.

"Can you identify the item within this bag?" I said.

It was a horseshoe.

"Has it been tampered with in any way shape or form?"

It hadn't been. I did that with every feat that night. The triple frying pan roll up I asked Diara's mother to come up to the stage to identify the items using her knowledge of the kitchen (she is a good cook after all). And for bending the steel bar over the bridge of my nose, I brought my Dad onto the stage...because if anyone is going to catch me in trying to put one over...it's going to be Dad. I've always been an extremely honest person, which is important for old-time *strongmanism*. I attribute a lot of that to my Dad, so he was the perfect person to bring up to catch me anyways.

After my portion of the show was over, I took off my gloves, caught my breath, grabbed some of the food that was out and sat where my families are seated and asked them how the show was while I watched Joe do his set. They said I did great. I was a success!

A day or so later I drove back down to Joe's stage to go over the footage of my show to see if there was anything to improve upon. There is always room for improvement, especially in entertainment and especially when you are new. Now I was going to hear what to improve from a seasoned and experienced professional. Some would dread it; I was actually looking forward to it.

First came the good news. I had good stage presence and charisma. This was great news to me because it's something you can't really learn. You seem to either have it or you don't and I'm apparently naturally likable while on stage. He did tell me a tale of a magician who would say to himself, "I love my audience, I love my audience, I love my audience" repeatedly so that it would change his physical state and give him more charisma. Here's a bit of advice, if you do this before meeting someone for the first time and you put yourself into a positive frame of mind, you will seem friendly because you are friendly. That will help you be authentic.

Then came the critique as he watched my show.

"Notice anything?" he said.

I tried to watch for what he saw. I was unable to see it.

I hadn't thanked the volunteers. Tsk, tsk, tsk on me. That's another piece of valuable advice that goes beyond the entertainment world. If you ask someone to do something, be thankful they did it. Just being thankful in general can pay you huge dividends. Gratitude is a very important trait for being successful.

Think about it, have you ever held the door for someone and they didn't thank you. What went through your head? Are you as likely to do something for them in the future?

I thank you, Joe, for that advice and for everything you guys have done for me.

A CORPORATE CHRISTMAS PARTY AND THE
LESSON LEARNED

I was cleaning my home office. Putting papers in the recycling and things I generally don't like doing so any distraction is a welcome distraction. And my cell phone ringing is no different in this case. The caller ID said that it's from somewhere in Pennsylvania.

"This is Eric, the Strongman, and owner of Eric Moss Fitness, how may I help you?" I answered the phone in my usual manner.

"Hi there Eric, I represent Julie from the company that found you on Gigmasters. We're very interested in your strongman act and think it would be a great fit for our holiday party."

Woohoo! Even though I technically had my first professional show for a Kiwanis club, since they were a non-profit, I only asked for the cost of the things I would be wrecking. The only reason I had even charged them was because I wanted to be able to say that I was a "professional" as in cash exchanged for services even if the cash was only enough to pay for my frying pans. It wasn't the same as actually being hired to do a show. I had already done a bunch of shows for nothing to get my feet wet, but I had set a goal of being a legitimate professional. This would become my chance.

"That sounds great! Can you tell me a little bit about the event?"

"Well the event is in early December and since we are going to have the entire venue renovated over Christmas break; beforehand we are going to put graffiti on the walls to make it look like a city street. Then we are going to have a street performers theme with circus acts and we think a strongman would fit right in. The people would come through in waves and you perform for them as a group. You'll be booked for three hours."

Interesting. Not really what I'm used to but I'm interested. If nothing this'll make for a great experience.

They were very interested in the frying pans and the nose bend and I told them that the frying pans were my most expensive feat (now unless I can find them cheaper, wrenches are the most expensive thing I bend). The nose bend I will only do once in a show because...well, it's not the most comfortable thing in the world.

The frying pans are always a hit though so it's hard for me not to include them in a normal show. I have a variety of objects I bend and they didn't want anybody to miss it so I limited it to a rotation of only a couple feats. Thick steel bars, frying pans, horseshoes and chains. I would do a feat approximately every fifteen minutes or so as the crowds moved through and when everybody moved into the next room they would announce my finale feat, which was the nose bend.

I agreed to the gig, signed the contract and received a check in the mail. The gig was two hours away according to Google Maps and I had planned to leave early because I liked to settle in ahead of time to prepare myself for the performance mentally.

It was a good thing I blocked out the entire day because it ended up being crazy. My house ran out of heat the day prior because the winter was brutal. We used up the oil faster than anticipated and knowing I wasn't going to be there in the afternoon to pay the guy had me in a bit of a panic. Luckily, he was able to come in the morning while I showered with air cold enough that I could see my breath. The oil guy got the furnace jumpstarted while I was in the shower, so it was just in the nick of time.

Driving over there I planned on arriving an hour early, but Murphy's Law kicked in. Apparently they were moving farm equipment during a long stretch of it and the people stuck behind the farm equipment were going half the speed limit and didn't have the presence of mind to go around them. The people behind them didn't want to risk passing multiple vehicles which made the rest of us get stuck behind the slowpoke...ugh. Then the rest was just standard traffic leaving me to arrive just in the nick of time.

I arrived stressed out from the rigors of traffic and just wishing I knew where I was supposed to be already. I went in and found the person I was supposed to talk to and apologized for being late (she said I wasn't late but in my head I was). It was a good thing for me they were running late. One of the other performers (a juggling unicyclist) still hadn't arrived. Well at least it wasn't me holding up the festivities.

One of the people there who was keeping the party organized walked me down this long corridor that was spray painted and had black lighting (cool) and led me into a big warehouse to my station so that I could get myself situated for the onslaught. I have a chair to sit in, a bunch of boxes behind me that I can place my bag filled with things to destroy for fun and profit and a giant rack for me to lean the steel bars against that were too big for the bag.

Above my station was a spray painted sign that said, "Strongman." There it was. It was official. I was a legit professional now.

I was told I could help myself to any of the snacks and drinks (non-alcoholic) and I saw a big curtain hanging from the rafters with a woman in a leotard standing at the bottom chatting with one of the workers of the party. With a bit of time to kill, I decided to introduce myself to her. As I got closer I overheard her talking about her time working in Cirque Du Soleil. Now she works as an aerialist and teaches people how to use "silks."

"Howdy, I'm guessing we're both part of the entertainment. I'm Eric."

"I'm Kendra. Nice to meet you. What do you do?"

"I'm the strongman," I said.

"You're the strongman?" She says with some skepticism.

"Yup," I say with a smile. I already knew where this was heading.

"No offense, but aren't you a bit small to be a strongman?" she said cautiously.

"Yeah I get that a lot. It's okay though, it makes me more marketable because it's proof that size isn't strength," I explain.

"So what are you going to be doing?"

"I'll be bending steel bars, rolling up frying pans, breaking chains and bending horseshoes. I sometimes do wrenches but I didn't bring any today...and at the end I'll bend a steel bar on the bridge of my nose," I said proudly while trying to stay humble by talking about it like its normal. Well it is normal I guess. Like the shirt that Greg gave me, which was what I wore that day.

"What's impossible to you is normal to us."

"Wow!" she said. "When you do the steel bar on your nose, can you tell me in advance so I don't miss it?"

"Sure thing," I said to her.

Time to get back to my station. Five minutes 'til the first wave.

Standing at my station somehow I felt like one of the Spartans in the movie "300." Ready for the first wave. Ready to demonstrate what I've prepared myself for through hard training. Only in this case it was to thrill the invading army.

I saw the first group of people moving closer and closer to me as they moved through the decorated warehouse. Grabbing snacks along the way and chatting with each other about how different everything looked. Now they were close enough for me to do my thing.

"Ladies and gentlemen may I have your attention just for a moment?" I projected my voice loud enough to capture their attention trying to make myself seem like a normal street performer.

When I looked up street performers on YouTube to research how to act prior to that day's show, the only thing I could really find were mimes. Very different from what I do and so I was essentially making it up as I went along. How would I have acted if I was a street performer looking for tips?

Well I probably would have tried to keep the costs low by only bending spikes which cost a lot less than frying pans and steel bars. Oh well, the more important thing was that these people have a good time after all.

That's what I was there for - to perform legitimate feats of strength for entertainment purposes.

A crowd of about fifteen people gathered around me.

"What I have here is a legitimate structural steel bar. It measures one inch wide and three eighths of an inch thick. I'm going to bend this for you lovely people today," I said holding it up as I handed it to one of the patrons so they could examine it for authenticity.

I put the steel bar on my leg and got into position acting like I'm about to bend it. Just before doing so, I held my hand up to my ear like I couldn't hear them and they took the cue and started clapping and cheering. Then I let the training take over and I bent it into a shape resembling the letter "U" and handed it to one of the patrons as everybody clapped at what they saw. Woot! First feat a success. They liked it. Now to keep the momentum rocking for another two and a half hours.

Second wave came through about the same size, I guess. This time I was doing a horseshoe and handed it to one of the girls there. Apparently she rode horses so she was thrilled to get the horseshoe. Lucky guess I suppose.

It was starting to come a little faster now. Uh oh, I hoped I had enough back up feats to make sure I wasn't left empty handed. This time I decided to do a frying pan. I went through my spiel.

"What I have for you people today is a legitimate Teflon coated frying pan."

I knocked on it so that it made a loud metallic noise signaling to the audience that it was not a rubber frying pan. Then I rolled it up and handed it to one of the patrons while everybody clapped before moving on.

One guy stayed behind, he was a gentlemen looking to be in his forties. He asked me if this is the only thing I do. I wasn't here to promote my personal training business and even if I was wishing to promote it, we were two and a half hours driving distance so it would make little sense to do. But he asked me a question, so I answered by telling him I'm a personal trainer by day.

"People like me don't have time to work out. I wish I did," he said making excuses. The same ones I hear time in and time out from people who don't achieve their goals.

I smile through my gritted teeth at him.

Time for a lyrical aside. My other superpower besides super-strength is my ability to freeze time, just like in *Saved by the Bell*. I can freeze time enabling me to add an extra hour or two in my day so I can work out. So you see I have twenty-five hours in my day instead of the usual twenty-four like most people do.

Of course, I'm joking.

I looked around hoping for something else to make this guy go away.

Nothing, and he was still standing there. Did he want me to justify his excuse? Or did he want to know the truth of the situation? Oh well, I guess I'll have to give him a quick lecture. I really didn't want to do this today.

"Lack of direction, not lack of time is what you have. We all have twenty-four hour days," I said, paraphrasing Zig Ziglar. Truth be told you only need about fifteen minutes at least twice per week if you follow the Pareto Rule. The Pareto Rule states that 80 percent of your results come from 20 percent of your efforts. If you focus on that 20 percent, it will pay dividends. Hmm, I guess I did add a bit of motivation in there but it probably wasn't what he wanted to hear.

But why would anyone want to hear why it's okay to make excuses? Hey, I didn't really want to be put in that spot to begin with. Maybe he'll actually learn from it, but it looked to me like he was in the excuse making habit. Look for ways to succeed, not reasons why it's okay to fail.

More waves kept coming and I saved some of the lesser known feats for some of the smaller waves that came into my area. I had a back-up feat of bending a pair of pliers backwards (I still wasn't a hundred percent on the technique) and ripped a hole in the pair of jeans that Diara had given me. A pang of guilt ripped through my chest because she had bought those for me. It happens sometimes during the shows because there is a lot of pressure and at this point my leg was really starting to feel it from the horseshoes.

The waves slowed down and I found myself free for a bit so I went to some of the local snack and drink tables and helped myself to some much needed nourishment while keeping an eye on my area. Doing feats of strength for a couple hours is a rough way to make a living but I didn't want to be caught abandoning my post. I was there to provide a service after all.

After a bit of time some of the planners came and got me to lead me into the other room for my finale feat. I didn't have a chance to grab Kendra but I'm sure she understood how this sort of thing happened. She wasn't exactly new to the entertainment industry after all.

I'm led to the area near the entrance of the warehouse where the rest of the crowd was to finish the party and it's announced to everyone that they were in for a special surprise. I thought there was going to be more than one thing but it turns out it was going to be my nose bend because the organizer knew what a rare thing that was.

Great! But I hoped to be able to tell them about how I became a strongman and what Greg did for me. I never got that chance because shortly after my nose bend the party was over and the cleaning crews came in. That was a bummer. I couldn't spread my message. I was just there to entertain.

I felt a bit like I was nothing more than a dancing monkey. I guess it was a good experience, but not one I would choose to repeat, not in that style anyways. Everything you do, whether you feel like it's a success or a failure directs you to your purpose. Mine wasn't to bend things to be someone's entertainment alone. I use the old-time feats of strength to deliver a message of positive self-belief and hard work.

As I drove home it was cold and dark. I knew I still had two hours ahead of me and it would already be late by the time I got home. I was tired and sore from all the bending and I realized, it's tough to make a living performing feats of strength. When the day was said and done it was a nine-hour workday if you factored in the commute.

Sometimes it takes a bit of experimentation to figure out what you really want in life or your career. If you use the analogy of walking down a foggy road you might not always know where you are going but as you move forward the scenery becomes more and more clear.

Yes, I like performing the feats of strength, but I wanted to be able to talk. I didn't want just to show off the fact that I'm strong and what I can do. I wanted to tell people what Greg did for me and to motivate and inspire people to be the best possible versions of themselves. I would later get that chance.

IRON TAMER TAKES MANHATTAN

I had gotten a text from Dave Whitley telling me that he was doing a workshop in New York sometime in January if I remember correctly. Dave has been critical to me in becoming a strongman and I try to absorb as much as I can from him and also support him whenever possible. Dave was my continued connection to the strongman world and it's important to surround yourself with like-minded individuals whenever you can.

Dave coming to my area was an awesome opportunity to not only learn from him, but also hang with the man at the same time. Dave was almost like an older brother who had been where I am, not that long prior and could relate some things to me that others couldn't. Like me, this was also his side passion and he ran a training studio.

"Iron Tamer, count me in."

With Diara living in New York I would have a place to stay so I wouldn't have to make an hour trip each day. Good thing, too, because New York can get a bit pricy at times.

I drove into the city from Diara's place, arrived a little bit later than I had expected since parking in the city is not the most pleasant experience. I found the address.

The door didn't look like the door to a training studio, at least none that I'd been to in the past, but hey; Greg's training studio looked like a welding shop in the front anyways.

I walked in and start walking up the narrow staircase listening for noise to lead me in the right direction. At the top of the stairs was a woman signing people in.

"Hi, I'm a guest of Dave's," I said throwing out the feelers. I wasn't sure how this 'check in' process was going to work since it varies from place to place when everything is privately owned.

"Ok hang on a second," She left the table momentarily to find the organizer.

"Hi I'm Kathy," the organizer of the workshop said while smiling. Kathy was an enthusiastic, bright-eyed woman with blond hair and seemingly endless amounts of energy and she was fresh off of the kettlebell training certification. She extended her hand to me. Behind her friendliness and wide eyed enthusiasm was a humbleness that masked her intelligence, albeit unintentional.

Kathy is a doctor of chiropractic medicine and an absolutely brilliant physician which I wouldn't discover till a bit later when I 'internet stalked' her. Behind her brilliance is a natural curiosity about the world and the human body causing her to have a relentless pursuit of knowledge, which accumulated quite a bit, turning her into an absolute whiz.

And she never told me she was a whiz. I found out later on from other people. I didn't tell her I was an old-time performing strongman either.

"Hi, I'm Eric," I said, smiling and taking her hand.

"Are you a friend of Dave's?"

Dave and I were traversing two separate but related fraternities; the strength training with kettlebells fraternity and the old-time strongman fraternity. Our paths crossed on more than one occasion and we had become friends through common interests (and not so common awesomeness :P).

"Yes, we are friends."

"Are you a high ranking trainer?"

"I've been training people in this style officially since 2009 and am well known in the community, but no I'm not high ranking," I said back to her.

"Awesome, can I see your kettlebell swing?"

The kettlebell swing is one of the foundational exercises utilized within the training system we use on our personal training clients. It's extremely helpful in injury prevention, power development and cardiovascular exercise. It's also helpful in strengthening people's backs. Kathy was enamored with everything she had learned about the kettlebell swing at the certification course.

"Sure thing."

I grabbed the closest kettlebell and proceeded to perform the swing.

"Wow, awesome! It's so fluid, powerful and explosive. You'll probably think my swing isn't so good."

"Well, let's have a look at it," I said. "I'm pretty good at picking out flaws...I get it from my mother." I told her jokingly.

She proceeded to perform as flawless a swing as I've ever seen. I couldn't find a single thing wrong with it. And I wanted to impress her with how awesome a coach I was by nitpicking the details that block perfection.

"Your swing looks great to me. I can't find a single thing wrong with it," I said honestly. Sometimes perfection is just sitting back and letting it do its thing.

I'm not going to fake being able to improve somebody.

Dave called everybody to attention. He started introducing himself, talking about the system, being a strongman and I was sitting there blending in with the crowd.

All of a sudden Dave noticed me and stopped what he was saying. "Eric? I didn't see you come in."

"I'm very sneaky, sir," I said trying to imitate the butler in the Adam Sandler movie *Mr. Deeds*.

"Everybody this is my friend Eric." I smiled and waved at everybody. Dave continued talking about his journey and some of the different concepts he'd created or taken from fellow instructors (while giving them due credit, of course).

Later on during the workshop we had covered an exercise called *the Turkish Getup* which is a feat of strength that old-timers sometimes used in the circus and also as a rite of passage. It involves going from a laying position to a standing position with a weight over your head. One of the feats Dave is known for is a combination of the *Turkish Getup* with sledgehammer levering. It's a nod to both the system of training he used and also to Slim the Hammer Man, a legend he looked up to.

I use the *Turkish Getup* as a regular part of my training and also as a physical test for people who want me to train them how to be a strongman.

If you want to be a strongman, you have to be strong plain and simple. If you can do a *Turkish Getup* with one hundred pounds, you are strong. When somebody asks me to teach them...I show them the exercise and tell them when they do it with the requisite weight of one hundred pounds then I will teach them what I know. Until then, I don't believe they are ready to learn the technique end. I try to show people the path I was on so they can learn from it, and I don't want people to specialize to early. It provides a barrier of entry for the people who are sitting on the fence and won't take it seriously.

Even though Greg didn't have the prerequisite for me, I had done it with that weight and built up the requisite levels of strength; enough where all Greg had to do was teach me take charge of my mindset and be able to focus the power I already had into the feat.

Dave asked me to demonstrate the *getup*. I grabbed a seventy pound kettlebell and perform the *getup*. Even though I'm capable of doing it with over a hundred pounds, there were still some form errors which Dave picked out even at seventy. But hey, he's top of the line at that. And even though I'm 'not too shabby' at the *getup*, even coaches need coaches. I'm a firm believer if you want to be successful at something, find someone who is qualified to coach you.

At the end of the first day's workshop we all decided to go out for food and drinks. I walked alongside the Iron Tamer as he was trying to get feedback on the workshop.

Thankfully I thought it was spectacular. Up until recently, Dave had run workshops for a company called Dragondoor but had left (along with several of the high and midlevel coaches, including myself). I told him I would have put it right up against any of the Dragondoor workshops I had been to.

Festivities were had later that night as we drank beer and ate barbecue. Some of the people who were there already knew me from some of the posts on Facebook and some were meeting me for the first time.

When it came time to cover the press portion of the workshop, I was still feeling the after effects of that car accident I had been in so hadn't practiced the press as much as I used to. I had neglected to tell this to Dave.

"I need someone with a big, singlehanded overhead press," Dave said even though he likely already knew who he was going to use.

He looks right at me, "Eric, you have a big press, right?"

"About average," I said. I didn't wish to come off as cocky or boastful.

"Let's see what Eric's 'average' press looks like."

I grabbed the seventy pound kettlebell which was a little less than half my body weight. I hadn't practiced pressing heavy and a lot was expected of me. I pushed the negative thoughts out of my mind and got into position.

I popped it up and proceeded to press it with confidence on my non-dominant side (also the side that didn't have anything wrong with it following the accident). I then did it with the other side (my dominant i.e. stronger side, but also the side that had felt pain). I pressed it up with confidence and also relief that it didn't hurt. It was submaximal, but I was also out of practice.

I hear someone out of the group say "I wish my press was 'average' ". Okay good, I didn't look like a wimp. :)

Near the conclusion of the workshop we had gone over a bunch of breathing methods that Dave had picked up from various sources. In the Mighty Atom's book, he was told by his mentor Champion Volanko that "Breath is life." The martial artists know it, yogis know it, La mas practitioners know it. When everything feels out of control, just breathe.

During one of the breaks, a woman introduced herself to me.

"You're Eric Moss, right?"

"Yeah."

"Hi, I'm a fan."

I smiled and probably looked confused.

"I have fans?"

The woman's name was Christina Devos and it would not be the only time our paths cross.

She had been a reader of my fitness blog before it had been taken down and it turns out a bunch of others who were at the workshop were followers of my writings, too. I heard many people talk and laugh about some of the posts, which were jabs against the dishonesty that plagues the fitness industry.

And for those who didn't know who I was previously, they would by the end of the workshop...because the Iron Tamer and I put on a strongman show.

Dave and I did feats in stereo. Steel bars, frying pans and I can't remember what else I packed. He did stuff with hammers and left me to bend the steel bar on my nose as the finale feat. I gave it to Dave while he hugged me and said Greg would have been proud.

Thank you Dave, and thank you to everyone else who saw what we do. We need to show it to grow it. So witnessing the impossible is critical.

Four of the women I met at this workshop, Kristin Dankanich, Doctor Kathy Dooley, Doctor Kathryn Mattson and Christina Devos, I would keep in touch with...and play a part in teaching them strongmanism in the not too distant future.

CONEY ISLAND HONORS GREG

"The strongmen are coming back to Coney Island babe. You want to go?" I asked Diara. I had taken Sarah the previous year and had a great time and wanted to do the same with Diara. It would be a shorter trip this year because Diara lived in New York not terribly far from Coney Island.

The previous year had been a great experience, the weather had been perfect and a large crowd had come to see the strongmen do what we do best. I was giddy as a preteen girl on her way to see a boy band even though I wasn't going to appear on stage. Not this year anyways.

We looked at the weather that day and it wasn't exactly good news. It was May and the weather was going to be cold and rainy. With this being an outdoor event and with some of the feats scheduled this was going to be especially bad news.

The day came and Diara drove because she's more familiar with the area than I am. We hit a ton of traffic. I tried to appear cool as a cucumber, but inside I was panicking that I might miss it. Mike Greenstein, the son of The Mighty Atom, the oldest living performing strongman was going to pull a Buick with his teeth at over ninety years old. When do you get to see that?

Almost never and I was nervous we weren't going to make it on time. Ugh, why is there always traffic whenever you are in a rush?

"There isn't a faster way?" I asked Diara. I have to be careful to control the tempo of my voice because if she senses my nervousness, it'll make her nervous, too.

"They're all going to be like this babe," she replied. I gritted my teeth and calmed myself down. There was no sense in getting bent out of shape about circumstances you can't control.

When we got there we rushed to find the area where this was all happening and found the platform. There was an act being performed called "The Milk Jug Escape" where amidst a song by a heavy metal band called Manowar a guy who seemed small for a strongman (smaller than I even) was getting handcuffed and submerged underwater in the milk jug where he would escape to the delight of the people in the audience. I hadn't realized it was actually magic. I guess I'm not the only one who believes that we should get along fine with magicians.

Personally, I love magic. I just don't do any of it and don't plan to because I know that if people know one thing is an illusion, they will assume everything I do is an illusion. It's human nature.

There was a strongman I was unfamiliar with named Gino Martino and he would do something that would get quite a reaction. His nickname was "Hammer Head" and we would quickly find out why. He took a board, put a nail on top of it and started hammering it into the board, using his forehead.

Diara screamed in shock and turned her head away covering her face with her hands. I laughed because she's seen me bend steel on my nose on several occasions. Yes, she is concerned each time I do it but this was the one to get the "OH MY GOD!" reaction from her and she wasn't the only one either. Gino also broke baseball bats with his head. I grinned and said "Awesome!"

I love this stuff.

The crowd was redirected from the stage to a more open area where the main event would occur - the vehicle pulls. Since it was a rainy day it was slippery and this was definitely less than ideal conditions. But you take what you are given and make it happen I suppose.

Chris Rider was the mastermind behind the Coney Island shows. Not just the coordinator but also one of the performers being one of the top guys out there today. He is a big strong guy with long red hair and a long red beard with an intensity in his eyes that some might be intimidated by. He's actually a really nice guy though that I would come to learn a lot from.

Today he was going to attach his pick-up truck to a chain that was clamped to his hair and pull it down the road. His nickname is "Hairculese" and he's called that because for one thing…his strength is on par with the ancient Greek demigod of similar name. The other is because he uses his hair and that's one of the things that make his feats unique. His hair is strong. It is strong enough to pull a truck and I happen to also know it's strong enough to break chains.

He started by putting some power into it, not as much as he could but as much as he could control so that he didn't lose his footing. His truck was a big one and even had people in it - but never the less it started to roll forward slowly but surely.

Once the momentum was going it was his. It became simply a matter of keeping it moving forward till the feat was finished.

Now came the part we were all waiting for. Watching a small man in his nineties pull a Buick with his teeth. This old man knew the secrets having been direct lineage to the Mighty Atom himself. He understood the concept of mind over matter and here he was demonstrating it.

He blanked out his mind, eliminated all other thoughts but what he was doing, gained purity of focus and pulled the car with his teeth…his real teeth, too.

And just like Chris Rider had done with his truck, this little old man got the Buick going and kept it going till the feat was complete. How often do you see this? It was a once in a lifetime opportunity - well to see it live and in person anyways.

He would later replicate the feat on America's Got Talent the following year causing one of the judges to jump up out of his seat in celebration. I'd say if you are causing that kind of reaction from a judge, you are doing something right.

After all the strength feats were completed I bumped into Slim. He eyed me with a curiosity like "Haven't I seen this kid before?" As of writing this, I'm thirty-three years old but could pass for twenty-three. I'm a bit of a baby faced steel bending strongman.

"Hey Slim."

"Hello, do I know you?"

"We've met before. I'm a strongman who was trained by Greg Matonick."

Slim often times has a steely gaze that could have inspired Clint Eastwood's trademark squint. It was a steely gaze that can make even the toughest of tough guys tremble. I had seen it many times before. In this instance his steely gaze softened as his thoughts wandered toward fond memories with my late mentor.

"Such a nice guy Greg was," Slim said with a kind smile. "…hell of a nice guy."

I nodded my agreement with him.

"He helped me through the hardest part of my life. I'll never forget him."

Off to my left I heard a woman's voice call my name. I turned and it was Kira, Greg's daughter.

"Hey!" I said as I hugged her. I was happy to see she was here keeping Greg a part of the community.

They were going to honor Greg on the Coney Island Stage and present the award to his daughter. Greg had been instrumental in keeping *strongmanism* alive. He was being recognized for helping to keep it going having played a part in Chris Schoeck's training and in my own.

Kira was called to the stage while a short impromptu speech was made about Greg, what kind of guy he was and his contribution to the community. While all this was happening there was some club solicitor to my right trying to get my attention.

"Psst, Hey," he whispered trying to get my attention. He held a flyer in his hand and was trying to hand it to me. I grabbed it trying to shut him up so that I could hear what was being said about my mentor. It didn't work.

"Shhh, they are honoring my late mentor," I whispered letting him know his advances were not welcome.

"Are you going?" he whispered.

My blood started to boil.

"No."

"Then can I have my flyer back?" Is he kidding me? I could feel my fists start to clench.

I directed my focus on this intruder, my eyes backed with restrained fury. I shoved the flyer into his hand.

"Now shut the hell up and get the hell out of here before I lose my temper and break you in half."

This time he took the hint and scurried off to whatever hole he came from, but the damage was done. It should have been pretty obvious with the way I was watching the stage during an award that this was not the best time to approach me. I understood trying to build a business, but it should be done while being respectful.

I sat there in the cold rain, while my blood boiled. I had missed a large portion of them honoring my mentor and I was angry because of it.

It would not be the last time he was honored, I will later tribute him on the AOBS stage, where he wanted me to perform to begin with. In the meantime, there was work to be done.

THE WRENCH AND THE HIGH SCHOOL FAILURE

One day I was checking my email and saw an email from Joe, the magician, who owns the magic stage that he and his wife run. Still actively performing he told me that they had been booked for an hour and a half for a high school senior send off and he hoped that putting my show in the middle of his as a sort of intermission would help. An hour and a half was a long time to do magic and it was a chance to help me out.

I had sought magicians out quite simply because they are the masters of diverting attention to where they want it to be. Another way to put it into contrast is that magicians want to divert your attention away so that you don't see what they are doing. That's what makes it an illusion. I want you to see exactly what I'm doing so it's raw, real and right in front of you.

Everything I do must absolutely be on the level in order to not wreck your trust. How would you feel if you found out I had gimmicked the stuff I did today to make it easier? You would probably feel if my feats were fake, then I would be a fraud and my message would then be lost.

I remembered the advice that Joe and Marco had given me in the short time I'd known them. I found the adage "a good magician never reveals his secrets" to be a false one, at least when it came to entertaining people. Now it was time to show them that I followed their advice and how much I had improved as a showman.

I figured since I wanted to be a motivational speaker that this was an excellent opportunity to do a short motivational message and test the waters a little bit. Knowing what I said to these students right before they graduated would be important, I had to capture their attention by putting on an awesome show that left them wondering what they could do if they put their mind to it. I give myself a quick affirmation to help me put on a great show.

The magic stopped, Joe walked off the stage, and my name was announced. Now it was my turn to rock the stage.

"Good morning high school seniors. I'm so thankful to be here because I believe this could be the most important show I ever do because as cliché as it sounds, you are the future and if anything I do inspires you to do something awesome, I've done my part. I want to thank Joe for putting on a great show and bringing me along. You know, I love magic and try to catch it anytime I get a chance. I love watching it, but it's not what I do. I'm a professional old-time performing strongman. I was the last student of New Jersey's Superman, the late Greg Matonick and I'm going to perform legitimate feats of strength for you today. What I have here is a bag full of various objects for me to bend, break and destroy. I promise you, nothing I do is fake. Everything I do is legit...is everybody ready?"

The class looked excited to see what I do.

I smiled and cued them to start my music.

"What you are about to witness is real, this is the old-time performing strongman experience and it's happening now," the deep movie trailer voice said over the loudspeakers.

Then the guitar riff started and it was on.

I ripped open a horseshoe.
I bent a 1inch by 3/8ths inch structural steel bar.
I broke a chain.
I was feeling awesome. Everything was going smoothly and I felt unstoppable until it was time for me to bend the wrench.

I had put the wrench into the bending position and started putting my power behind it.

Nothing happened. I regrouped my mind and put more power into it.

Nothing happened. I put as much power as I could, my vision shook, I had tunnel vision and still nothing happened.

Uh oh.

Even though failures do happen from time to time and it's "understandable because we are human" I would lose the respect of my peers. Even if I didn't actually lose respect, I would still feel like I did. But I was also here to put on a good show.

Time to address the crowd.

"This wrench is putting up more of a fight than I initially thought. I can keep going but I don't know how much longer this is going to take. I'm leaving the choice to you. I can keep going or I can move onto the next feat. What do you want me to do?"

I gave them the choice of what they wanted to see.
The audience indicated they wanted me to move onto the next feat, which was a triple frying pan roll up.

Even though I wasn't technically defeated since I hadn't called it quits I still felt as though I had because it didn't go in a timely manner. After I finished with a steel bar bent over the nose and beckoned them to do something amazing with their lives; I walked back stage amidst applause and the congratulations from the magician and his wife who had set me up with this gig. I still felt as though I was defeated.

I sat backstage wondering what Greg would have thought about me not being able to bend the wrench and it haunted me. Although the main purpose of the show was to try and inspire them to do something great, which the point was taken, I still felt as though I had let my late mentor down.

What would Greg say if he knew I hadn't been able to bend it in time? With every performance I pay tribute to him and I like to think that he sits up in the heavens, looking down on me beaming with pride. Would he have been proud? I wished I knew.

The guilt haunted me to get even stronger because the discomfort of another botched feat is something that I really dislike. The triumph over steel feels great. It feels like accomplishment. And the roar of the crowd as I perform for them feels amazing. Even after that show where I had "failed" I did a Q&A session where the students could ask me anything they want. I got the expected questions like how much could I bench press; but the question I wasn't expecting was from the girls "Are you single?"

When I answered "no" it was met with booing (and on the day after Diara's birthday too). Still got my looks, I guess.

Anyways even after the questions and answer session there were still two seniors who wanted to talk to me before leaving for class so I stuck around to chat with them a little bit. I told them how disappointed in myself I was for my inability to bend the wrench in front of the school. What they told me changed this story of failure into a learning experience. They told me "If anything, it showed us that what you did wasn't fake."

If I had precut the wrench...I could have bent it no problem. But since part of being a strongman is to do nothing which intentionally deceives the audience, to do something like precut the wrench would have violated my code and my mission statement of integrity.

The other lesson I took from that is to recognize the bigger picture, without letting the sub goals distract from the main goal. Don't let one failure ruin the entire show. The point of me being there was to put on a great show of inspiration mixed with authentic feats of strength. All of the feats were authentic and judging by the crowd reaction and the fact that they wanted more (always leave them wanting more) I'd say the task was accomplished. The crowd had forgiven me for being unable to bend the wrench before I could. Is there anything in your own life that you are having trouble forgiving yourself for?

Oh and if you are wondering about that wrench and if I ever got it. Yes, later I took the thing and put as much power as I could for as long as I could and snapped it. I put it into a shadow box to give to mom and dad as a Christmas present along with the first line of this book.

"I suppose I got my first lesson in perseverance from my parents."

AOBS DINNER ONE YEAR AFTER GREG

I was out of town assisting at a personal training certification and I saw that I had a new message from Dave Whitley.

"Chris Rider wants to get into contact with you," Direct and to the point. My interest was piqued because Chris is a top-level strongman, one who coaches many of the other top level strongmen and coordinates some of the big events. Like the Coney Island Strongman Spectacular and also the Association of Oldetime Barbell and Strongman annual Reunion Dinner, where I had been introduced to this art form and where I had met Greg.

"Send him my number," I texted back, anxiously awaiting Chris to contact me. I wasn't sure what he wanted, but I had a gut feeling.

Word had gotten around to the other strongmen about how active I was. I was friends with a lot of these guys on Facebook and would post every time I was doing a show. Well, almost every time. I had hoped that I was doing right by the profession, and being Greg's last student, I felt like I had an added responsibility to keep his name alive in the strongman world.

A couple minutes later, I got a call from a number I didn't recognize, from somewhere in Pennsylvania. That must be him. I ducked out of the room.

"This is Eric the Strongman and owner of Eric Moss Fitness," I say in my usual way of answering the phone.

"Hey, Eric, this is Chris 'Hairculese' Rider, how are you doing today?"

"I'm good Chris, how are you?" I replied.

"I'm doing fantastic. Are you planning on going to the Association of Oldetime Barbell and Strongman Dinner this year?"

"Absolutely."

"Well, I'm coordinating the Stars of Strength show that happens on the second stage of the dinner and I'd like you to be a part of it. Are you interested?" What a stupid question...of course I'm interested. ☺

"Absolutely," I said.

"Great, how are you with bending steel on your nose?"

"I did five-eighths of an inch round structural steel a couple weeks ago at my St. Jude's fundraiser. It was a bear, but that's what I'm capable of."

Nowadays, I prefer to do reinforcing bar.

"Excellent, I'm thinking about having you do that one and the triple frying pan roll up with Dave Whitley at the dinner. It's good to have a wide variety of feats - the last thing you want is ten guys doing horseshoes. Not many do the nose bend so that's what I'd like you to do."

"Sounds good to me Chris," I smiled into the phone.

We spent a bit of time chatting about *strongmanism*, various feats, Greg, Coney Island and a bunch of other stuff that escapes my memory. I walked away from that conversation with a bit more knowledge on various feats and the hope to at some point be coached by him. I had been in a bit of limbo without Greg's tutelage and wanted to improve myself by learning from other top guys. If there was someone who could help me improve the feats, it was going to be Chris.

I gave Diara a call and excitedly told her the news.

"That's great babe!" She was happy for me but I'm not sure she understood the full gravity of this.

This event was where I originally met Greg and it was almost one year to the day of when Greg passed. I was going to be able to honor him there, the best way I know how, the way he taught me.

The day inched closer and I went to Walmart and picked up the frying pan set. I took a picture of it for Instagram and Facebook noting the ad copy on the box saying that it was built for durability with a five year limited warranty and my claim that it wasn't likely to survive the strongman dinner - not when Dave and I void the warranty by doing what we strongmen love to do. What Greg taught me to do.

The day came; I arrived early to try to get my head on straight ahead of time because I knew how emotional this was going to be for me.

The last time I was at the Marriott in Newark for the strongman dinner two years prior I was a broken man, trying to survive a failing marriage and meeting my mentor, my guide and my friend - who would provide the light at the end of the tunnel and would completely change my life before he was taken from me.

Now I was here as a strongman, the last student of Greg Matonick, almost a year to the day from when he passed - to honor him by gracing the stage with what he taught me. It felt surreal to be there. It was going to be like coming full circle.

I met with Chris and Dave to go over some new feats and the day's show. I wandered around talking to the various strongmen who were there while I waited for Diara's arrival. I was going to need her because of how emotional this was going to be for me.

Was I going to fall apart on stage?

Was I going to command the respect of the other strongmen there?

What if I botched the feat? No, I couldn't think like that.. It was going to happen. It must happen.

And where the hell was Diara? She was taking forever.

She wasn't even really late, I was just getting antsy because of the day and I tended to get that way prior to a show.

She arrived looking absolutely beautiful. Oh boy, I was going to have to fend the other guys off of her.

I introduced her to some of the guys and spent time with her otherwise she'd feel completely out of place. At the same time I was trying to keep an eye out for either Greg's wife or daughter just in case they were there so I could give them the steel bar that I was going to bend with my nose in his honor.

Dave and I were going to share the triple frying pan roll up. It was originally Dave who I saw do it which let me know that *strongmanism* was actually something and he was the one who introduced me to Greg so it was symbolic. He was going to go on before me, we would share the feat, and I would finish with the steel bar on my nose.

Dave did his part of the show with the sledgehammers in front of the stage because he was concerned with the space. Now it was time for the frying pans and he told the story about the first time I saw him do the triple frying pan roll up feat and invited me to the dinner and where I met the strongmen. He gave the short version of my getting started on the journey of the strongman with Greg as my guide.

"I think I speak for both of us when I say this one's for Greg," he said as he got into position to roll it up. He wasted little time and started crushing it down in the style of Dennis Rogers, who taught him the feat. He broke off the handle and grabbed the second frying pan and handed the feat over to me.

I took it without saying a word and crushed it down and started rolling it the way Greg taught me, around the frying pan that Dave just did. Without a word, I held it up overhead to absorb the applause of those who witnessed it. Dave then took the third frying pan and started to roll it up and I handed him the first two so he could complete the triple frying pan roll up feat. He held it up and the clapping started again. He walked off the stage to let me take it from there.

I stepped up onto the stage without saying a word. I didn't say a word because I was emotional. Chris was emceeing and took a moment to tell the audience about how I was mentored by Greg, who was always at the dinner and told them I had the nickname "The Last Son of Krypton" to pay tribute to him.

It was time to pay tribute to a good man, to Greg, who was named New Jersey's Superman by Don Polec of *ABC News*, who taught me how to bend steel. Since I was his last student before he passed away that's where the name came from.

My official stage name is quite simply - Eric Moss.

Chris told them the same thing I told Chris about learning from Greg and it was time for the nose bend. I felt the weight of the structural steel bar pushing down on my nose.

"Are you ready, Eric?"

"I'm ready Chris."

Chris asked for them to give me a countdown which is what I do to both build suspense for the feat and also to clear my head of any negative thoughts that might stop me from doing this. Nothing would stop me from doing this. It was inevitable.

"10" I breathe in positive crackling energy.

"9" I breathe out all negative thoughts and emotions.

"8" I breathe in positive crackling energy.

"7" I breathe out all negative thoughts and emotions.

"6" I breathe in positive crackling energy and feel it reinforce me, filling me with unstoppable power.

"5" I breathe out all thoughts but the task...the task of bending structural steel on the bridge of my nose.

"4" I breathe in, filling me with power.

"3" I breathe out ridding me of weakness and distractions.

"2" I breathe in, ready to explode with power, the power that Greg taught me I have.

"1" This one's for you, Greg.

I pulled hard, feeling the weight crush down on my nose. It didn't bother me. It was in front of the other strongmen, including Slim the Hammer

Man and the sons of the Mighty Atom, in front of Greg who was there in spirit, looking down from the heavens.

The next thing I knew, I was holding the bar up overhead and everybody was clapping. I was still doing the breathing and I was sure it looked like I was doing it because I had exerted myself. I was doing it to hold my emotions together. I had come to honor my mentor and to do so was huge for me. Thank you, Greg. I bowed and walked off the stage to let the show continue. Chris Schoeck was up next, the guy Greg had taught before me.

I walked through the audience to get a drink of water from the back of the room and I saw an older gentlemen who exuded a very positive and friendly vibe sitting in one of the chairs. He motioned me to come over to him.

"You did very well up there," He said with a smile.

"Thank you, I appreciate that," I told him.

We got to talking and he had noticed that I was quite a bit smaller than many of the strongmen out there. He knew it was not about the size of a person that determines his or her strength; it was about the mindset of freeing yourself from self-imposed limits so you can demonstrate your true power. He knew this well having studied the psychology of elite athletes for longer than I had been alive.

"Are you far from Montclair State University?" he asked me.

"Not really, why do you ask?"

"I'm a professor of sports psychology there. I'm writing a book on mindset and I would love to have you come in and talk to my class. My name is Dr. Rob Gilbert," He extended his hand and I shook it.

He handed me a piece of paper. I read it.

October 5, 2013

Dear Strength and Fitness Enthusiast:

I NEED YOUR HELP!

I am currently doing research for a book on extraordinary feats of strength.

But here's the catch - I am trying to find stories about people who were not strong enough, big enough, or trained enough to do what they did.

I am looking for people who credit their mental powers or their mental training (for example meditation or visualization or imagery) for their extraordinary strength feat.

We've all heard the story of a tiny woman lifting a 4,000-pound car because their child was trapped underneath. I am looking for true-life stories like that.

If you have a story for me, I want to include you in the book. Call me or email me!

And if you know of another person I should contact or book I should read or any other resources I should look into -- please get in touch with me.

My email address and phone number are listed at the top of this page. I would be grateful for any help you can give me.

Thanking you in advance.

Rob Gilbert'

I talked to him about trying to artificially recreate the stimulus that allows people to do extraordinary feats of strength as well as some of the affirmations and other things Greg taught me. The thought of being mentioned in his book was very cool to me. (Side note - seeing this book you are reading now is something I'm looking forward to as well.)

"Very nice to meet you Dr. Gilbert," Somehow I knew from day one that he would be a good person for me to know. I would learn from him and meet some incredible people through him.

After chatting with the good doctor, we exchanged information and I found the "Man of Steel" Sonny Barry in the lounge. One time when I was with Greg after I bent a steel bar on my nose, he told me that of the people he's taught, I was the second fastest to progress in the old-time feats of strength. When he told me this I was floored, but also curious who the first one was. He told me it had been Sonny and I said I didn't mind coming in second to him because he's a "terminator". Greg and Sonny were very good friends that bonded through strength and mutual respect from arm wrestling.

Sonny had commented on my nose bend and the fact that I only used a shop rag for padding. He had been extremely impressed by it, which was awesome to hear. For one thing, I had told him how impressed I was with him when I saw him punch through a piece of wood that seemed about as hard as the wood on my deck and the difficulty of some of the short bolts he bends. The other reason was because here we were two of Greg's students with mutual respect. I hadn't been involved in the strongman world very long, but I think I had done well for myself. I plan to go far with both the might and the message and each step I take is a step forward in the right direction.

I later met up with Diara at the bar as I told her of everything that had gone on that day.

Later that evening, I watched some of the other strength performances which were happening as well as other shows. That evening a bodybuilder was going to do a posing routine on the main stage wearing next to nothing dancing around flexing his muscles.

I thought to myself, "Respect for the amount of work that this guy has put into his craft, but it's definitely not my thing. My thing is bending steel and using it to inspire people." Watching that bodybuilder doing his posing and dancing, I kind of felt like I was at a Chippendale's Show. Yeah it's not my thing, not that there's anything wrong with that.

Leaving there that day, having paid tribute to Greg while wearing the shirt he gave me, I decided to retire that shirt and put it with the rest of the things I have of Greg.

It would not be the last time I would wear it though, there was definitely more to come.

DR. ROB GILBERT

Somehow I knew that Doctor Gilbert would be a good person for me to know. I didn't know exactly why, I just knew. I figured it sounded cool to be interviewed by a professor of sports psychology and would make me sound marketable both as a personal trainer and as a strongman. I even used it in some of the free presentations I do for local businesses in the "who am I and why should you listen to me?" portion of my presentations that I do for business as well as the mini-bio in my email signature.

"Subject Matter Expert" to the Department of Exercise Science and Physical Education at Montclair State University in the areas of Sports Psychology and Peak Performance. Well, it is true after all. Part of being a strongman is taking advantage of whatever leverage points you already have.

What I hadn't realized was that as much as he might learn from me, I would learn more from him in return. Probably tenfold.

In addition to being a professor of sports psychology - he was also a motivational speaker, a mentalist, an author, the creator of a success hotline, a mentor for motivational speakers and some other things I haven't learned about him yet. He was someone who I could learn directly from, who could captivate audiences of athletes to get their head in the game. He would also help me get my head on straight when it came time to do my talks and just be a good person in general.

One day I got a call from him asking if I would be available in the afternoon. Most of the time I was not because I have a personal training studio to run, but this particular instance I was free. I brought a frying pan, a piece of flat stock structural steel, a horse shoe and a piece of round stock structural steel (for the nose bend).

I met him in the cafeteria of a high school where the football team was having a banquet and getting ready for a pep talk. Once again I arrived early and met the good doctor outside where he introduced me to some of the coaches there.

There was a buzz about the place and I was unsure of what was really going to happen. Dr. Gilbert was leading the charge and all I had to do was await instructions and do what I was trained to do, what I was born to do, what I was called to do.

Dr. Gilbert began and I watched as he got the athletes' spirits up relating stories of top athletes into his speech. This was no ordinary motivational speaker. An ordinary motivational speaker would go up there and just kind of talk. Dr. Gilbert was getting them up and moving around, playing games and basically doing anything he could to make the message stick through a variety of means. Then he started talking about the mindset of the old-time strongmen and the idea of giving it your all.

"And I met somebody that makes a living by giving it his all," He said introducing me.

He asked one of the athletes to try perform one of the old-time feats of strength I had lined up saying, "If you can do this I'll pay for your college education."

Oh crap! I watched in fear that this might actually happen. Here's the thing and it goes to the mindset of the old-time strongmen.

If a woman, who has never touched a weight in her life, can pick up a car to save her child...what are you capable of doing?

The feats of strength are not impossible. The fact that I do them routinely as part of an entertaining show is testament to that fact. Someone who is desperate and/or properly motivated can summon up an incredible level of strength.

The offer to pay for an expensive education can be a highly successful motivator and combined with the fact this was a trained athlete who has the confidence that comes with youth...well let's just say this was a very risky wager for the good doctor to make.

So I watched and he wasn't able to do it in that moment in time. I let a sigh of relief out and now it was my turn. I ripped through the feats of strength like I had done when called to action and it came time for the finale feat, which was bending the steel bar on the bridge of my nose. This time when I did it I bent it around into the fish scroll (the one that resembles the ribbon).

"You should bend those and give those to cancer patients," one of the athletes says to me as he inspects it after the show while I'm grabbing a bite to eat. I couldn't help but smile that this guy was on the same page as me when it came to the idea of using strength to help people. Perhaps one day he would do the same as I was doing. People needed to hear the message of internal strength anyways. The more people who know this... the better.

I walked out with him to the parking lot to get his take on what I could do to improve and he had a couple suggestions. One of the common things amongst strongmen is challenging members of the audience and inviting them to be a part of the feats of strength. An example of this is when Slim "the Hammer Man" Farman would challenge the strongest looking guy in the room to try and pick up his challenge hammer by the end of the handle. He would then pick up a hammer weighing twice the weight of the challenge hammer. When I asked him if anyone had done it, he told me nobody. I've attempted Slim's challenge hammer. I was not successful at that moment in time...but one day I will.

I don't normally challenge people during my show because I don't want people to fail. I understand the concept of getting them to realize how difficult something is but I don't want anyone to feel that they are inferior to me because I can do something and they can't. The themes of my show and my motivational speeches are set up as "We all have this amazing power, the power to do incredible things, to be happy and to get what we want out of life. We just need the focus to do so, the strategy to tap what we already have inside of us."

Outside in the parking lot, I told Dr. Gilbert the reasons I don't challenge people and why I also don't include magic.

"You are a very humble person, Eric," he said to me.

"And it's good you stay true to your craft, but remember what it's really about," he said.

"What's it about, Doc?" I replied

"Here let me show you something."

He performed some magic and some mentalist routines that left me bewildered and amazed, wondering how he did that.

"It's about the way you make people feel," he said.

Point taken. People associate feelings with memories. If the feelings are positive, if they remember being amazed, inspired or motivated then you will trigger good feelings when they think of you. Imagine for a moment that someone thinks about you. Do they feel a pang of anger? Or do they feel good when they think about you? Which do you prefer?

Later on he would invite me to do what I do for his college classes and I would be able to sit in.

Go back to college? Interesting proposition. I knew that I could learn a thing or two but the thought of showing the class what I do was an intriguing one. I wouldn't be able to do it in every class because of the demands of my personal training studio but I jumped at the opportunity both to learn and to perform. At that point in time I needed exposure and practice, even more so than I do now.

I drove up to the college and walked on campus with my steel bars, my frying pans and my horseshoes looking for the building he told me. It was a bit of a long walk since I didn't really know where I was going. I have a young looking face, so I probably blended right in with the college crowd and nobody questioned what I was doing.

I got to the room a little bit after class started and nervously poked my head in there.

"Come on in, Eric," he said with a smile.

I found a seat that was a little bit off to the side where I could put some of my different things on the floor without tripping anyone.

The good doctor, now spoke as the college professor who was there to do more than simply "profess," - was there to not only teach but to inspire (and one I wish I had when I was back in college). He showed video of a football coach who had instructed his athletes not to pay attention to the scoreboard during the games.

His reasoning was that you should play the same, no matter what the play is, no matter what it says on the scoreboard. Give it your all, every play, and the scoreboard will take care of itself all on its own. When the scoreboard takes care of itself every game, so does the win versus loss ratio. It worked for that coach.

What if you lived your life the same way?

Once again I was used to demonstrate the example that he was talking about of giving it your all, all the time.

I was introduced to the class as "The 'great' Eric Moss". It felt strange to be introduced that way since every time I had done it before I did it as a joke. Well now it was time to live up to the hype of being great. If you raise the standards and decide to be great, don't just think you are great. Be great.

I took the steel bar, I treated it like it is barely within my limits even though I had cut a length that I would be able to do without too much fuss. I went through my breathing sequence and hulked up and went into the bend at full force to make 'the impossible' look easy. I did that with every feat and got a great reaction from the students that day. I answered the questions that the students had for me after class and wrote my email address on the board to stay in contact.

Afterward, as we were walking out, one of the other professors who had seen what I do commented on how I was and it was the first time I had heard this.

"What I find truly terrifying is how quickly you get in and out of that zone. It's only a matter of seconds and you're in it. Then in another couple seconds you're back to normal."

Interesting. I hadn't been described as terrifying since Halloween.

What's also interesting was that I had gone to that class that day to teach, and learned something myself in the process. I find it's often times like that. Even with writing this book.

Those were my first experiences with Dr. Gilbert. They were not my last.

TWO AMAZING MOTIVATORS, A ONE LEGGED TAP DANCER AND MYSELF

I had done a couple performances for Dr. Gilbert's classes and had great responses thus far. Normally the gigs are for the hours when I'm not at work because of the demands of my personal training business. That's a tradeoff of running two business' at once, but hey, when the opportunity to do a show or to be able to speak arises I try to be there.

Fortunately, in this story I was available.

I got a phone call from Dr. Gilbert asking if I would be able to do what I do during a talk he was going to be doing at the Yogi Berra Museum for some sports teams.

He had told me he was bringing in some other guests, too. I wasn't sure who, but I'm not opposed to sharing the stage as long as what I do is framed correctly. (This wasn't going to be like sharing the stage with 'snails having sex'.)

I was coming from my personal training business so I wasn't able to leave as early as I would have liked. I had warned him in advance that would likely be the case. It wasn't going to be a problem since there were other guests, all I had to do would be to wait for my cue and he was able to improvise anyways.

I wasn't completely sure where I was going since the campus was a large place. It was hard to read the signs in the dark so I asked one of the people in the parking lot if I was in the right place. I was.

I grabbed my stuff and walked through the empty hallways listening for the sound of the good doctor's voice. I heard it and moved in that direction trying not to make a lot of noise.

I found the door and tried to sneak in - in full view of every one who may have thought it unusual that I was walking in with steel bars. I didn't carry my stuff in a case yet since I hadn't found anything that all of them would fit into.

There was the stadium style seating where the audience was seated to watch Doctor Gilbert's giving his talk as well as the seats where his guests were seated. There was only one other guest that I saw since the other one was still on his way. I hadn't known of either of them prior to the show.

In one of the seats sat a stylish young man. I whispered an introduction to him as I shook his hand, not wishing to distract the crowd from Dr. Gilbert's talk.

When I shake someone's hand, I look them in the eye and give them a firm handshake. I don't look them up and down. So before I sat down I didn't notice the metal pipe that this guy had sticking out the bottom of his jeans. I noticed it when I was already seated and checking out the rest of my surroundings. He had a peg leg. His name was Evan Ruggiero, a student at Montclair State University who had appeared on *The Ellen Show* for being able to tap dance despite being an amputee.

The other guest walked in, he was a very tall African American fellow. He walked over and introduced himself to us. It was pretty obvious judging from how tall he was and the nature of his build that he probably had a talent for basketball. I would discover that day he was also a very talented speaker.

Dr. Gilbert signaled me that I'll be up in a few minutes. I took this opportunity to get myself loosened up. I knew that doing so would put their attention on me so they could get ready to watch what I do. Dr. Gilbert started talking about 'believing in yourself and giving it your all' and said, "And I met someone that gives it his all every time he's on stage, here he is, the great Eric Moss."

"Good evening everybody."

This time Dr. Gilbert was going to be somewhat of an Emcee for me.

"Eric, is going to do some strength tricks for us."

"Silly doctor, tricks are for kids. What I'm going to do are legitimate feats of strength."

"Why don't we leave the jokes up to me," he said smiling. "What is that in your hand?"

"This is a piece of structural steel, measuring one inch wide, three-eighths of an inch thick," I replied.

"And what are you going to do?"

"I'm going to bend it."

"Do you have any doubts that you are going to be able to do that?"

"Nope."

"Great, let's see it."

I held the steel bar up so everyone could see it clearly. Then I put it into bending position and motioned the crowd to make a bit of noise. They started cheering as I set my mind right.

I bent it around into the U shape, getting the ends as close together as I could. Dr. Gilbert brought up a volunteer to try and open them. They struggled, unable to move it. He told them they could get any member of the room to try and undo my feat. They picked their friend, still unable to do it.

"You should have just asked me," I said smiling.

The next feat was the wrench. I held it up giving a short introduction about it being a drop forged steel wrench. Put it into the bending position; put my power onto it.

SNAP! This wrench broke, slamming my knuckles together. Hurt a little bit, but not bad. Hearing the snap though gave a great effect and I could hear the involuntary reaction of amazement coming from the audience.

If I could snap it each time I would, but you don't always know what the wrench is going to do. It seems half the time they bend, half the time they break. I never know which it's going to do going into it. They can be unpredictable at times. And the lifetime warranty on those things doesn't mean anything when you don't use it for its intended purpose. I know of other strongmen who have tried.

After that I did a horseshoe and a frying pan and sat down bumping fists with the other guests who had been unfamiliar with me and were surprised at what I do. I still had one feat in the hopper, which was going to be left for last. The nose bend.

Dr. Gilbert continued. He took a ball, bounced it and bounced it again. He used it as a metaphor for bouncing back from adversity and asked his next guest to give his story. Evan Ruggiero stood up and gave his story of chasing his dream despite the adversity he faced.

What I would recommend you do is to go onto YouTube right now and look him up. It's okay, put the book down and check it out.

Evan had fallen in love with tap dancing from the first time he saw it. He practiced and developed a high level of talent for it that was created purely through desire and passion. One day during a recital he had a pain in his foot, had it checked out by a doctor who recommended going to a specialist. It turned out to be bone cancer and due to complications from it, he lost his leg.

That didn't stop him though. He had a leg made out of a metal pipe and the leg-maker had said, "When you can dance, I want to come see."

Then Evan went through this routine where he started clapping to a rhythm, then putting his foot down to the rhythm and next thing you know, he's full on tap dancing and putting on an excellent show. He even did it while singing "Dead or Alive" by Bon Jovi. Evan was not dead, he was very much alive as he was unleashing his passion and using it to inspire this group.

Awesome! Pure awesome right there. It was something that made me sit back and realize just how fortunate I was to not have to go through what he did. It also made me sit back and reflect on how epic it was that I got to witness this and it was because I had become a strongman that opened this opportunity. Being a strongman opened a door to a beautiful new world, and I walked through it with curiosity and amazement. It's one of the many stories that led to this book.

"That was incredible," I said to him, giving him my seat to sit in. I wasn't about to let him think for one single solitary second that what he did was anything short of amazing.

Dr. Gilbert continued, connecting the dots and making sure the message was getting through to the audience. There was still plenty more to be had though. Up next was Michael Spence.

Michael stood up, towering over everybody. When he started talking, his message was bigger than he stood. I find it difficult to even describe how powerful he was as he spoke but I immediately thought to myself, "I need to be able to talk like THAT if I'm going to get through to people." The presence he had and the story he told held everybody captivated. If this guy wasn't established or well-known, he will be. I would learn later that he was trained by Dr. Gilbert to do that and he was a star in the making. I knew then and there, it wouldn't be the last time I saw him. And I was right.

Before I had a chance to talk to him and congratulate him I was up again, to do my last feat, which was bending steel on the bridge of my nose.

I got the crowd to give me a countdown to build anticipation.

"10" - Here we go again. Breathe in.

"9" - Breathe out.

"8" - Breathe in.

"7" - Breathe out.

"6" - Breathe in.

"5" - Breathe out.

"4" - Breathe in.

"3" - Breathe out.

"2" - Breathe in.

"1" - I pull...hard.

"Rawr!!!!" I yelled out as I pulled the steel bar down hard against my nose. Hard enough to properly convey believing in yourself and giving it your all. If you don't believe in yourself, if you don't pull hard and give it your all...it's not going to happen. Plain and simple.

I finished the bend by "fishing" it. Turning it into a scroll resembling the ribbon shape that started Rebar to Ribbons.

After I took my bows and thanked the audience I remembered Evan's story of chasing his dream and not succumbing to cancer so I walked up to him.

"I want you to have this. I hope that it becomes a symbol of the strength you already possess and reminds you of how strong you already are whenever you look at it," I said to him. He looked surprised, shook my hand and thanked me.

The audience members, the teachers, coaches and students were all shaking our hands and taking pictures with all of us and when their individual teachers started grouping their teams for the busses, I took that moment to walk over to Michael Spence.

He appeared to be deep in thought. I decided to interrupt it anyways.

"I just wanted to tell you, you were amazing up there. Very powerful."

He thanked me and told me the same thing. It would not be the last time we met.

I went straight to Diara's place that night. With her, her mom and her sister in the kitchen making a plate for me they asked me how it went.

"You need to check this out."

I showed them the YouTube video of Evan tap dancing with his peg leg. His story, seeing him doing that, hearing Michael speak and hearing Dr. Gilbert actually in action and coordinating all of us, was an awesome experience.

One that I would not have been a part of had I not opened the door when opportunity came knocking. Opportunity to be a part of amazing things doesn't come along every day. But if they do, it just might be worth checking out.

Life provides many opportunities that you may not be aware of if you aren't keeping your mind open to new possibilities.

SPEAKING OF DR. GILBERT

Later on I would keep in touch with Dr. Gilbert and knew that if I was going to get better at the motivational speaking part of it, I would need to be coached. I figured to get my show the best it possibly could be, having the right coaches to really sharpen the blade would be the best way to go about it. I also really wanted to make sure people got the message about the power within to and that I'm not up there to show off how strong I am. I go on stage to inspire people with my strength and my message. That was the lesson I learned from that corporate holiday party. Speaking is something I need to be able to do in order for me to feel right.

I knew I needed a coach to be able to really dial in my motivational speaking. Dr. Gilbert had been generous in providing me with advice and opportunities. I knew he had worked with both Dennis Rogers and another strongman named Russell Jones. So I sent him an email.

"Hey Doc,
I don't know if you check your email in the summertime but I was wondering if you would be willing to mentor me in motivational speaking. I really think I have a lot of potential to reach a lot of people by fusing strongmanism with motivational speaking; I just need to tap into it and rock it,

Hope all is well."

His response copied and pasted right from my email:

145

"Hi Eric,

I WOULD LOVE TO!!!

Let's get started as soon as possible.

Currently, I am in a rehab in Lincoln Park.

I had knee replacement surgery two weeks ago and now I am here.

This is not fun.

Thanks for keeping in touch!

RG

Sent from my iPad"

The part where he said that he would love to in all caps was the exact response I was looking for. If you want to get good at anything it helps to have a mentor who can steer you in the right direction - like Greg did teaching me how to be a strongman, like Chris would eventually pick up where Greg left off, I could dial in this area too. Dr. Gilbert recognized the bigger picture.

As he would say later on, "If I teach you to motivate and it changes a life; I will have been a part of that change and that makes me feel great."

Those may not have been his exact words but the underlying lesson is still the same. The domino effect of how you treat someone, how you make them feel or what you influence them to do sends a chain reaction that makes the world a better place or a worse place. What kind of effect would you like to have on the world?

Dr. Gilbert gave me the number to his room and I gave him a call. He sounded like he was a bit out of it because of his knee surgery. He was staying full time in the physical therapy facility so that he could get the best care and get back on his feet in the shortest time possible.

One of his themes during his talks is giving it your all. When it came to his rehabilitation on his knee, he was acting no different. I was thankful that he was willing to take time out to let me talk to him to learn from his experiences. Some people in his position might not have been so generous.

So a couple days later I get this email from him:

"Eric,

Would you be free this Thursday at 7:15 pm to work with me?

We will be speaking to the football team at Kean University.

RG

Sent from my iPad"

I jumped at it because it was a great opportunity to see the things he told me put into action, this time from the framework of having been told the rhyme behind the reason. I was surprised though, that he was already speaking so soon. I mean it was literally just a couple days ago that he was full time in the therapy facility and now he's going to be prowling around the stage in front of the football team? Well, Doc is a smart guy so he knew what he was doing.

So I spent the night before cutting and cleaning my steel and packed my bag with other supplies. I only needed to pick up some reinforcing bar and forgot to get it before my evening session at my training studio, so I would have to get it someplace between there and Kean University. Fortunately Home Depots are everywhere so I pull off the route to get some.

After I found the rebar, it was time to head straight over, but when I tried to set my phone to get the address for Kean and the room number (where on the campus it was), the phone decided to crash. I couldn't even turn it on. I was completely out of contact from the Doc, from Diara and anyone else who wanted to contact me.

Oh boy, not good. Not good at all.

I found my way to Kean University, but it's a big place. I was carrying around my steel bars and other things I was planning on wrecking in a guitar bag. Walking around the campus asking where I might find who I was looking for was a timely process and the straps from my guitar bag were cutting into my shoulders. There were several things going on that night. I had gotten the run around for about an hour 'til I made one of the students working in the Student Success Center make phone calls to find the person who could find the coaches I was looking for who could direct me to where I was supposed to go. Finally he found the coaches and one was on his way to get me. Only he also went to the wrong place.

All in all, I had arrived on campus an hour early, but after all the running around I was finally in the right place - five to ten minutes late. Had my phone not crashed, I would have been able to contact the right people no problem, but it was what it was and you use what you have available to you right then and there. Even though I was a tad late, Doc didn't bring me on 'til a little bit later in his speech, but I missed the way he opened it and I was hoping to get new insights on the beginning from seeing how he started.

I walked into the room trying not to draw attention to myself and made my way to the front of the room along the wall. I saw Coach Mike Tully who would guest speak and I also saw Michael Spence, who had changed his hair cut so I didn't recognize him. I got my stuff ready for quick access for when I was needed and borrowed someone's phone to tell Diara what had happened. I got a drink of water because after all of the running around, I was thirsty and wanted my full strength to be able to perform when the time came.

"So I want you to be able to go all out, and I met somebody who makes a living by going all out every time…" That was my cue.

I stood up, gave my arms and legs a quick shake out to get the tightness out of them and introduced myself.

"Good evening….I was trained to be a professional old-time performing strongman by New Jersey's Superman, the late Greg Matonick."

I did some of the feats including bending the flat stock structural steel. Doc challenged the coach to open it after it was bent. The team cheered and heckled him a bit at the same time and then a couple players had a go at it. I always got a bit nervous when this happened because these are peak athletes involved in a sport that involves quite a bit of power. Nobody did it though. I gave a short talk about the mindset that's involved and rip through some of the other feats and I take a seat again, to the congratulations of the other guest speakers.

I continued to watch Dr. Gilbert prowling around the stage with control over the audience, getting them involved with the show and I could see that he is masterful at his craft. I have much to learn and I'm able to see that now. As Dr. Gilbert would say there is more to being a "wow speaker" than simply going up there and being a talking head. This audience was engaged and involved.

After a bit of time, it was Mike Spence's turn to speak. He stood up and delivered. Coach Mike Tully started laughing. Since this was a serious topic, I asked him what he was laughing at.

"He's so good," was his reply. I agreed. Mike Spence definitely had a knack for it.

After the other guests did more speaking it was my turn to go up again. This time it was for my nose bend. I went up and got my countdown so I could clear my mind and when it was time, I pulled the thing down hard on my nose, finished it off and absorbed the applause from ninety-two players and twelve coaches. It was a great feeling. I talked about the mindset involved with doing such a feat and made the announcement that I was planning on setting a world record. I didn't say exactly what I was going to do since I didn't really have it figured out, but I had an idea and that idea would come to fruition. It is inevitable.

The nose bend was saved for the end to leave a lasting impression and several of the players stood up to say what they were going to do to make this a powerful year for their football team. To me this signified the message had sunk in and it was nice to know I was a part of the process that led to them pledging to do the best they possibly could.

After the speech was over, I found myself surrounded by the athletes, each one towering over me, picking my brain on what goes on in my head and how to reach the mindset. I had a flashback when this happened, to middle school and having been surrounded by people who were picking on me for being quiet.

This time, they were eager to learn from me. I could be wrong about this, but I feel like the generation that came after me is more respectful than the one I was a part of. But hey, I'm on the outside looking in.

As we walked to our cars, I noticed that Dr. Gilbert was back to limping and I asked how his knee was.

"It's killing me," he replied. The good doctor had turned it off while on stage and didn't let anyone know he was injured. When there is a job to be done it has to get done.

It was late by the time I finally got home and ate something. The next day I checked my email and saw another email from Dr. Gilbert. The subject line simply said, "Wow!"

The message body went as follows:

"Eric,

You were fabulous tonight at Kean!

Want to know if you ever give a great talk?

Just look at how many people want to speak with you AFTER the talk.

They were all over you!

Great job,

Dr. Gilbert

Sent from my iPad"

It made me happy to see that things were improving for me. I am always looking to improve the way I do things. Seeing the way the athletes reacted to me with my own eyes and having it confirmed by Dr. Gilbert told me I was heading in the right direction.

Is what you are doing working? Find ways of measuring the immeasurable and provide mile markers so you know you are headed on the right track.

I knew I was headed on the right track simply because I was putting the right coaches in place. I could learn from their successes and their failures. Sometimes they have big steps forward and sometimes they stumble. When they learn from it and teach it as long as I was a good student, I could do great things with it.

EIGHTIETH BIRTHDAY FOR A LEGEND

I was lying on Diara's bed while she organized some of her end of the school year things. My cell phone alerted me to a text and was a welcome distraction. It was a text from the Iron Tamer Dave Whitley.

"How far are you from Pottstown, PA?"

I Google mapped it.

"About two hours…why?" I asked, curious at the random question.

"You want to go to an old man's surprise birthday party?"

There was only one old man who I knew of in Pottstown. The legendary Slim the Hammer Man and he was turning eighty.

Oh man, just about anybody who is anybody in the strongman world is likely going to be there, to pay tribute to a man who has been inspirational for just about all of us. The one who originally made me aware of the power within. He was one Greg so often spoke of as an example of how to approach a feat as he taught me to believe in my own power.

Long story short, Slim the Hammer Man Farman is a big deal and I was honored and a bit nervous about whether or not I was even worthy to be able to attend his birthday party. What I saw here would be amazing.

151

I packed a piece of reinforcing bar to bend on the bridge of my nose…just in case.

When I got there it was a warm summer's day and I saw many of the strongmen who I had seen performing at the Association of Oldetime Barbell and Strongman Dinner.

I saw a new face, though I had seen him before on YouTube. His name was Jonathan Fernandez.

Sometimes in my spare time I look up different strongmen on YouTube to see how they run shows, how they introduce feats, etc. I see a lot of people who do things like "popping" phone books (a method of tearing a phone book that makes it very easy and is considered by legit strongmen as 'cheating,')

With so many strongmen who aren't the real deal I clicked on Jonathan's video and thought to myself "alright let's see what this joker is doing."

I quickly realized "this joker is legit" when he mentioned Greg's name as he put a horseshoe into his mouth and bent it. Whoa.

In conversations with Chris, I discovered that Jonathan was one of his students and we befriended each other on Facebook. Today he was here to pay tribute to Slim and to meet many of the guys.

Meeting for the first time in person, we chatted for a while with a mutual respect for each other. We got pulled off course when Slim started dropping some knowledge bombs.

It was time to put our listening ears on.

"The difference between a human and a machine is a human will push 'til he thinks he can't go any further. An hour later, you'll find him dancing the old boogaloo. He didn't really give it everything he had. A machine like a crane will pull and pull until the machinery breaks down. The difference is in your mind. If your machinery hasn't broken down you haven't truly given it everything you got," Slim said.

We, young men, sat intently listening to the wisdom and experience from the legend. I was reminded of my failure at bending the wrench and it haunted me. I didn't say anything about it though.

Sometime between the food and the upcoming feats of strength, I bumped into Dave and we talked about various feats we were including into our shows. He threw a bit of a curveball into the conversation.

"I'm glad you're here."

"I am too, Iron Tamer"

"I don't mean here as in here, I mean here as a strongman. If *strongmanism* is going to continue and grow we need more people who can talk in front of an audience."

"I hear you. You know I honestly feel like I was meant to do this. I've had a desire to be in front of an audience but I'm too small to be a pro wrestler and I'm not that talented of a musician"

Dave grinned and nodded in agreement. Dave had been in rock bands previously as a guitarist and had also performed as a professional wrestler with a vampire gimmick.

One thing about being a strongman is that many of us are perfectly content using the feats of strength as a method of exploring our own limits. Many have no desire to do a show or ever to perform and I believe that is one of the reasons *strongmanism* is so rarely known. There is something inside some of us, that gives us the desire to perform on stage and *strongmanism* happened to be the vessel to do it.

According to Jerry Seinfeld, more people fear public speaking than death and therefore if you are at a funeral you are better off in the casket than giving the eulogy. Personally, I get excited whenever I have a show coming up.

Not only is it enjoyable for me, but it almost feels like a moral obligation. The strongman feats when backed with a message provide a powerful opportunity to change lives through the strongman principles of self-belief, envisioning the result and powerful focused action. Dave and I arrived at this conclusion individually and would soon discuss it.

Later that day some of the other strongmen started doing horseshoes and cards. I debated grabbing my reinforcing bar from my car, but sat back instead to watch what they were doing. If my time came, I'd have it ready. Jonathan bent a coin with some small wraps. Russell Jones blew up a hot water bottle filled with confetti.

Strongmen were doing what strongmen do best.

The anticipation was killing me as I followed Chris back to Slim's place after the party. I had seen it on DVDs, but it's different when you are there.

This is Graceland for the upcoming strongman.

"Oh man, I'm headed to Slim's dungeon!" I thought to myself.

I arrived and saw a broken down old truck. This truck, even though it was old and overgrown, had a very familiar look to it. It was the truck the Mighty Atom had driven with his family in his later years when he was giving health lectures (in a way kind of like what I do with my fitness presentations today). Then came the tour of the dungeon.

Wow! The things I read about, the things I visualized in my head were here. The steel that the Mighty Atom had twisted which took every ounce of power he had. One of the thick boards that both he and Slim had driven nails through. A horseshoe wrapped by the Mighty Atom himself.

There were pictures of the different strongmen who had crossed through there over the years. I found one of Greg on Slim's wall. I knew that Greg had been here and I believe the dungeon had inspired Greg to decorate his gym in a similar manner.

"Hey Slim," someone called out. "What do you think of this guy?" he said pointing to a picture of Chris Rider.

"Oh, him? I don't like him," Slim casually said.

I glanced at Chris and saw a slight grin through his beard as he awaited the punch line.

"He was my wife's boyfriend, and when I see him I think to myself, if he's her boyfriend...how ugly must I be?"

Everybody cracked up.

Slim enjoys his jokes. A bit later we were all summoned to his hammer levering platform.

When Slim did his hammer levering he made sure to do everything the same each time. He is very big on ritual and the reason is it helps your mind settle down and focus on what you are doing. It's kind of like having a subconscious mental checklist which allows you to go all out. It was systematic.

We watched intently as he went through the motions with a relatively large size hammer mentally preparing himself. He got in the position he used for levering hammers, his opposite hand blocked out the head and took it away in his mind so all he had to do was pick up a light stick. He breathed in and readied himself.

And then he threw it at me!

It wasn't real… it was a toy hammer! It was one of Slim's practical jokes. He didn't get me as good as he had gotten other strongmen though.

Someone had reminded Slim that when he was younger he had vowed he would still be able to do the hammers when he was eighty. Today would be that day.

First the challenge hammer. Slim brought out the twelve pound challenge hammer and asked if anyone wanted to try it. Dave Whitley did it and succeeded. So did Chris.

"Any other volunteers?"

I thought to myself, "Don't pick me. Don't pick me. Don't pick me." And I heard Dave say, "I think Eric should give it a go."

Damn it, Dave! ☺

Alright, set my mind on what I was doing so I didn't look like a fool.

I choked up the handle as best as I could. Man this thing was thick around…I could barely get my fingers around it (yes, I know what she said).

I had done this before, but not with a hammer this difficult. I set my mind on the task put the power into it and my fingers slipped off.

Every attempt and my hand slipped off of it. I wasn't able to do it and was looking like a fool in front of the other strongmen. I was pissed at myself for my inability to do the feat.

Despite my shortcoming, nobody made me feel like a fool as I thought they might. I just wasn't as far on the journey as they were.

After showing me how difficult this feat was, Slim pulled out his signature double twenty-four pound hammers. Two hammers, each one twice the weight of what I had attempted.

And he levered them. Twenty-four pound hammers on thirty-one inch handles, which equates to…a lot. It was something he had done in front of an audience of eighteen thousand people in Madison Square Garden, setting a world record in the process and cementing himself as the king of the leverage lifts.

That is quite a feat for anybody. And Slim recreated it at eighty years old. Let me say that again.

EIGHTY YEARS OLD!

He was doing feats of strength that are *untouchable* at an age when people have a hard time just standing up out of a chair. It's one of the things that fascinated me about *strongmanism*. It transcends age.

Afterwards, we all ate dinner at Slim's place and I had a chat with a fellow named George Smiley, who is always supportive of the strongmen. He knew Greg and had seen how far I had come from being a wide-eyed fan to a wide-eyed fan that was now performing strongman feats in shows professionally.

This guy had been there chatting with Greg at the Coney Island show recollecting how Greg was saying he couldn't wait to get his back surgery so he could start riding his Harley again. His Harley that he was customizing with bent horseshoes as the gear shifters and bent wrenches decorating it. I very much would have liked to see him on his bike.

I told him I remembered Greg said he wanted me to be a better strongman than him and that I was doing what I could to make it happen.

"It's a tall order, Greg, but I am ever working to improve what I do; strongman feats with an inspirational message to make the world a better place."

Even if I don't reach the levels of strength that Greg had, at least I'm the strongest I can be.

As the night went on people started to leave 'til it was just Slim, the Iron Tamer and me. I was a bit worried I'd outstayed my welcome but I wanted to catch anything I could as Slim told us stories and gave us relationship advice (Slim would buy his wife, Shirley, flowers A LOT). Flowers can be costly, but back rubs are free. ☺

"You guys want to see some footage I took of the Atom and me?" Slim asked…knowing what the answer would be.

"Sure."

When Slim turned around to walk inside, Dave and I mouthed the word we were both thinking to each other, "Yay!"

This was like a Yankee fan being invited by Mickey Mantle into his living room and watching footage of him and Babe Ruth that he had taken on his own camera. Can you imagine?

We walked in as Slim tried to use his VCR. Not everything had been converted to DVD yet and Slim was looking through his private collection of things to show us that would blow our mind. This was literally the only place where these videos could be found.

"This stuff is going to blow your mind," Slim said to us excitedly as he searched through his tapes. Slim 'The Hammer Man' Farman, as much of a legend of this stuff as he is, was still a fan in his heart. Especially of his mentor the Mighty Atom.

He was looking specifically for footage of the Atom as he was biting chains apart…link by link. He never found it at least not before I left later that evening. What I saw instead was still awesome.

The Atom putting up a barbell overhead weighing about ninety-five pounds…with one finger. Slim bending five-eighths inch reinforcing bar on the bridge of his nose during a show in Alaska. Slim and the Atom performing at Madison Square Garden when Slim set the world record in front of eighteen thousand people. Footage of old shows with another strongman named Jack Walsh who would go on to teach Stanless Steel (a strongman who is capable of bending coins…and picking up a platform holding three people with just one finger).

And footage that would seem like it was nothing, but I found it mesmerizing.

It was footage of the Atom selling his homemade health products from his truck (the same truck that was in Slim's yard). Washing his hair and demonstrating that he could eat the soap (somehow the Atom was able to make soap out of egg whites).

I'm not sure what it was that made seeing video of a little old man sitting behind a table selling soap so mesmerizing. I think it was because the Atom was almost mythological to me and because it showed this superhuman as a regular man doing regular man things. He was human after all, except when it came time to do the feats.

COACH CHRIS "HAIRCULESE" RIDER

After Chris saw me perform at the Association of Oldetime Barbell and Strongman Dinner and saw my stage presence, we developed a bit of a friendship through the bond being a strongman can provide. We would chat about various things about *strongmanism*, showmanship, self-promotion, the history and everything in between.

Chris, the natural teacher that he is, would every so often start dropping knowledge bombs over the phone and whenever he did this I would run and grab a piece of paper to write it down. Success leaves clues and if I'm ever going to be the strongest I possibly can, I need to learn and apply all that I can.

In addition to that, I wanted to help keep *strongmanism* alive, not just by performing at the highest-level possible, but also by having other students spread the word. A number of people had approached me after shows, or upon seeing the videos and I had used the alleged old-time rite of passage of doing a getup with one hundred pounds as being the entryway before I would teach people to be a strongman. That's how strong I was before I went to Greg and I didn't know how to start anyone out who didn't have that entry level of strength.

Greg didn't have that prerequisite. I started off relatively strong, considering, and that strength had needed to be focused and cultivated.

When I started with Greg, I was a broken man in need of a guide and a friend. He took me from a broken man to a strongman in less than a year. I took the wisdom from him after he passed and used it to become a professional. If I was going to take it to the next level though, I needed another guide. And yes, I wanted to take it to the next level. I want to be primo.

I'm a strong believer in having coaches, but they have to be the right coaches who can connect you to what you need to learn and have your best interests at heart. Chris would become that coach.

I knew Chris was a businessman. Greg had a hard time ever accepting money, even though he should have and I wanted him to. In Greg's mind, he loved teaching strongmen and shouldn't accept money. I had told him that it's a rare thing and he shouldn't refuse to be paid just because he enjoys it. I wanted to help him start a school for strongmen and was going to start planning it after I became successful. We never got that opportunity because heaven called him earlier than expected. I felt guilt at not being able to help him do that and grow this relatively unknown skillset.

I would get that opportunity with Chris.

One day I was leaving my training studio, when out of the blue I get a call from Chris Rider.

"Hey, I want to run some things by you," he said into the phone.

Curious, I asked him what he was thinking. I figured he wanted to book me for a show or something.

"I think the world needs to have more strongmen and I believe that personal trainers like you might have an interest in learning how. What if we did a workshop in your studio? The host would train free. Do you think you could connect me to other personal trainers?"

Redemption. This was not only an opportunity to take my skills to the next level, round out my training and relearn some of the things I had forgotten, but it was also a way to bring *strongmanism* to some of the people who I knew were fascinated by it.

"I'd love to help you out. Is there a strength prerequisite?" I asked, testing the waters so I knew whom I could invite.

"No strength prerequisite. I will take anyone, at any level and give them an action plan. How far they go is up to them."

Oh good, because I know some ladies who are going to love this stuff. I knew from previous experience that summer is a slow time of the year for personal trainers and I figured summertime would be the best time. In the end I was wrong and I wasn't able to fill the workshop because of scheduling conflicts with the potential students.

I marketed it hard in an effort to fill the workshop. It was important to me to build *strongmanism* since it had saved my life by providing me with hope. I was upset by the fact that I couldn't fill it.

"Hey Chris, I'm sorry I couldn't fill the workshop. I understand if you no longer want to hold it in my facility. If you are still willing to do it, we can try rescheduling one on a later date." I sent him the text. I was nervous he was going to say he didn't want to work with me.

"I think you did a great job marketing it. Sometimes these things are just timing problems. But let's get your strongman skills up to speed first. I'll need your help coaching."

I feared I had lost my opportunity, but Chris saw the greater picture and I think he recognized coaching ability in me.
Coaching is a skill, and it's a skill I believe I naturally had from my very first personal training client.

I could be wrong on this, but I think one of the reasons Chris wanted to work with me was because I'm a coach myself and also because I am highly grateful for my time with Greg and I always try to give credit where credit is due. I don't pretend to be self-taught in strongman feats. I am the product of the teacher-student relationship coupled with hard work.

The teacher teaches, the student learns and applies the lessons. I am successful because of that equation and I pay tribute to the ones who I learned from. That is part of the reason for this book you are now reading.

So it was time to go down and meet Chris at his place, and learn from potentially the best strongman coach living today. There are a handful of coaches out there now, including names I look up to, but I'll be honest I haven't learned from them so I can't really compare, but I know from personal experience that Chris is an excellent coach and I've come a long way moving toward the next level under his tutelage. I'm not the only one either. Success leaves clues.

I drove down to his house in Pennsylvania, about a three-hour drive if I remember correctly, and I wasn't fully sure where I was going.

I pulled up to his house and saw him waiting outside by his pick-up truck.

"How are you feeling? Are you fatigued from the road, need to eat or anything like that?"

"I'm good, Chris."

Travel can be fatiguing but part of being a true professional is being able to bring it under any condition. I didn't want to waste time either, knowing how valuable Chris' time is.

"Good, let's take a trip." We jumped into his truck and headed to a local flea market. "Now when you are going to do a show it's important to pick your battles. It needs to be within your comfort limits so you can make it look good, but still be a respectable feat. The other reason for flea markets is because it's not what you make, it's what you keep."

One of the reasons I save wrenches for higher paying shows is because wrenches aren't cheap unless you find them cheap. Neither are frying pans, but I like the reaction I get from them and they are always a hit.

We got to the flea market and discussed our personal branding and how it's important to be the brand all the time.

It's actually a funny thing how the reputation of a strongman precedes them. Even at my family parties one of my cousins who I watched grow up, brought her boyfriend to a family party for the first time. She says to him, "This is my cousin Eric, he can bend horseshoes."

At a graduation party another one of my cousins told all of his friends that I bent steel and when I got there, they all wanted to see my promotional video. I don't know if this happens in other professions but I find it curious that I'm sometimes regarded like a mini-celebrity, even within my own family. Curious, but I love it nonetheless.

Anyways, we walked around looking at various vendors to find some stuff that would be respectable and look good since he knew I wasn't too shabby at bending wrenches. I never tore decks of cards (Greg didn't like tearing cards, so he didn't really do them or teach them to me)

We needed a good place to start and we found a huge box of cards that would provide me plenty of practice material. He taught me hand positioning in his truck and figured out how many cards was within my comfort zone - about thirty cards. That was the starting point for me and the goal was a full deck.

The action plan was to add one card per week. Barely enough to seem like it was making a difference, but those small successes when repeated consistently over time lead to bigger successes. You don't always notice the progress happening but then one day you arrive. Funny how that works, isn't it?

We later stopped at a tool supply store to find different nails and bolts as well as wood for driving nails through. Incremental progression is key to building yourself up at a sustainable rate. Build upon your previous successes.

On the way back from shopping with Chris, we were discussing a bit about the mindset of a strongman. He told me,

"When you go to the place that you need to be, you need to have no regard for personal injury. Can you go there? When I'm doing a feat I'm going from a state of complete calm to unloading everything in a snap. If you don't get the feat, and they don't carry you off stage, you aren't letting the audience down, you aren't letting me down or Slim down or Greg down…the only one you need to reconcile with is yourself."

And at this point, the wrench that had beaten me at that high school senior send-off still sat upon my coffee table at home. It bothered me and I knew I would eventually do it. I would do it for myself.

After going over some footage of one of my shows, we headed to his place to shift some of my biomechanics on the different feats. In particular, I was struggling with bending nails because I hadn't practiced them. It was the same thing with driving a nail through a board with my hand.

"Get into a fighter stance, so you can put your entire body into it. Gather your chi and go into it," he said as he demonstrated his preferred position for bending nails.

"Position it so that it has nowhere to go, but to bend to your will," he said as he adjusted my wrists. The nail came easier than it had before. Admittedly, I was stronger than when I first learned it from Greg, but this positioning was great. I knew from the feel of it I could put it into my shows. Stronger than steel, tougher than nails.

We tore license plates, phonebooks and cards. With ripping things, there is a focal point where you need to concentrate the power rather than dispersing it throughout the entire feat. It's actually like any goal; concentrate the power where it matters most.

I left Chris' that day with a new found respect for his coaching because I had experienced it first hand in person. I had an updated action plan for my shows and for being a top-level strongman and speaker and now it would be easier to market the Coney Island Strongman workshop. I could show my progress in real time by ever improving myself as a strongman and not settling for less than my potential allows.

With the power I have inside and the power I'm still only now learning to tap, it is simply a matter of time and application.

BENDING STEEL FOR COPS...AGAIN

I included this story just because it's a fun one. Whenever I tell this story to cops they get a kick out of it.

It was the weekend following my thirty-third birthday. My parents had called me because they wanted to take me out. They said, "Any place you want to go."

I don't get to eat Thai food nearly as often as I'd like. I love Thai food. I love all sorts of ethnic foods but have a special penchant for spicy foods and Thai is a rare treat for me.

So I chose Thai Nam Phet, a restaurant in the town where I grew up. It had been there for years and I had eaten there on more than one occasion and enjoyed it each time I went.

When I order Thai food, I ask for them to make it extra spicy, with a side of the spices so I can make it even spicier. Thai restaurants will often times hold back a bit because a lot of people like to think they are tough, take a bite, it's out of their comfort zone and they send it back. I don't send it back, but they didn't know that yet.

So we have a great time, Diara and I, my sister and her boyfriend and Mom and Dad. Afterwards I stopped by my parents' home, then as the night went on we started to get a bit tired and decided to call it a night.

Diara and I headed home and I pulled off at the exit to take one of the main roads through town. I saw a police cruiser in the rear view mirror.

Then its lights started flashing.

Oh boy, what did I do?

I pulled over, opened the window and took my keys out of the ignition and turned on the cab light. Put yourself in the shoes of a police officer, you pull over a car at night and it's dark. You don't know if that person is carrying a gun or something. Turn on the cab lights and they feel safer. You always feel safer if you know what's ahead.

The police officer walked over to my window. He was a young guy and I didn't get a bad vibe from him. He seemed like the kind that you can joke around with.

"Good evening, officer."

"Now don't worry, you aren't in any trouble or anything."

"Oh good."

He greeted Diara and poked his flashlight around my car; I guess checking for anything suspicious and he saw my guitar amplifier in the back seat. I use it as a makeshift PA system during my strongman shows and hadn't taken it out yet. Thank goodness, otherwise I would miss out on this fun story.

"Are you a musician?"

"I used to be; now I use it during my old-time performing strongman shows."

I can see the question mark form over the police officer's head.

"What's that?"

Now it's time for the same shtick which I use whenever I explain it. Since

166

strongmanism is so rare, most people have never seen it or even heard about it. Well I guess that's going to change tonight.

"I bend steel bars, rip open horseshoes, break chains, roll up frying pans, drive nails through boards with my hands all as part of a show, much like you would see a magician do, except these are authentic feats instead of illusions, and I give a motivational speech with it."

"Get out of here, you really do that?"

"Yes I do," I said smiling. I enjoy seeing childlike curiosity in adults...especially adults who have guns and badges :)

He shines the light on my girl, "He really does that?"

"Yeah it's real," Diara says while rolling her eyes at what a cartoon character I am.

"Do you have any horseshoes here?" That was my cue; we're going to rock this. It's on baby.

"I don't know, let's find out...I'm going to open the door and exit the vehicle." I said announcing my intentions.

I opened the back seat of the car looking for horseshoes; I didn't find any. I had a thick piece of structural steel leftover though. It would have to do.

"I have this. It's a piece of structural steel. You want me to bend it?" I said holding up it up in the light where he could get a good view of it.

He examined it with his flashlight and felt the weight of it.

"Get out of here, you're really going to do that?"

"Sure if you'd like me to."

"Wait, before you do that, can I call my friend so he can come see it?" he asked me excitedly.

"Call whoever you want, the more the merrier." I said laughing. He was the one with the power. He was the one who would decide whether or not I would get a ticket after all. But I knew after this, I most likely wouldn't get anything.

167

Besides he hadn't even told me what I was pulled over for yet.

He pulled out his radio and said something into it.

"He'll be here in a couple minutes," he assured me.

"Not a problem," I said, awaiting my turn at around eleven at night with a stomach full of spicy Thai food ready to bend steel for some cops on the side of the road.

He walks over to Diara's side of the car and taps on the glass startling her,

"I'm sorry to embarrass you like this, miss."

"Oh, it's ok," she said assuring him. She was posting this on Facebook because it was becoming a funny story. She'll deny it, but I'm positive she gets a kick out of me being a cartoon character.

The other police cruiser arrived with its lights flashing. I must have looked like a serious threat to have 'backup' called.

He introduced me to his friend.

"He's going to bend this piece of steel."

"Get out of here; you're really going to do that?"

"Yes sir I am really going to do that."

"Oh I can't wait to see this."

"Ok first, I want you guys to inspect this to make sure it's legit and not tampered with, I'm going to just take my keys and cell out of my pocket and put them on the trunk of my car." I said again announcing my intentions. When doing a feat of strength it's important to minimize the distractions just like the first thing Greg told me when I first started training with him.

Then after they've checked it I took the bar from them and put it into the bending position and did a mock hulk up that I do mainly for effect. I acted like I was going to do it and right before surging down, I looked up and said, "You ready?"

"Yes."

Then I simply blanked out my mind and surged downward doing what I had been trained to do, switched it around to adjust the leverage after the first bend, then crushed it down into the "U" shape.

The flashlights danced back and forth as they clapped while holding them in their armpits.

"Dude, that was awesome. How did you get involved with this?" The officers called me "dude", like I said, I get a kick out of seeing the childlike curiosity in people. Especially people who can give me traffic tickets. I told them the story of me being a personal trainer and how that led me to train with Greg before he passed and currently Chris as I hand them the steel bar so they could see it better.

They passed it back and forth before handing it back to me. I handed it back.

"Yours to keep my friend, now you can use it as a reminder of that one time you pulled over that one guy that bends stuff," I said smiling.

"You have a website?"

"It's being worked on, but just type my name in YouTube and you'll find me." One of them went on his iPhone and looked me up.

Side note, my website is StrongmanEricMoss.com.

"Yeah that's me," I said pointing at the image on the screen of me bending steel bars on the bridge of my nose.

I joked around a little bit with them before they handed me back my license and registration and told me I had a headlight out and that was why they pulled me over.

When Diara and I got home she was tired and wanted to go to sleep. My adrenaline was soaring at this point. I don't want to sleep, I felt like jumping up and down on the bed.

Two weeks later I was driving home in the daylight. I came off the highway on the same road through town. Again there was a police cruiser behind me and its lights came on.

Oh boy, what did I do? I had fixed my headlight.

I pulled over in the exact same spot as two weeks ago and did the exact same thing where I roll the window down and take the keys out of the ignition.

"Good morning, officer."

"Good morning, license and registration, please."

I handed him my stuff. He poked around my car looking for things that might be suspicious.

"What do you do?" He asked. Well since you asked...

"I'm a personal trainer with a studio in Parsippany and on the side I'm a professional old-time performing strongman." The dice had been cast.

"Huh? What's that?"

I go through the description of what a strongman show entails.

"Get out of here, you really do that?" He said. Deja vu. Was word getting around the department?

"Yes I really do that," I said smiling, knowing where this was headed.

"Do you have anything here?" I had recently purchased a couple frying pans and they were on the floor of the passenger side of the car.

"I have some frying pans; I could roll one of them up if you like."

"Yeah, that would be awesome!"

"Sure thing, I'm reaching down to grab the frying pan and I'm going to exit the vehicle." I said announcing my intentions.

He took a look at the road. It was a bit busier during the daytime than it was at eleven o'clock on a Saturday night.

"Honestly, I don't want you out here; it's too dangerous for you."

"Well I've never done the frying pan while seated before, but hey let's see how it goes," I said shrugging.

I showed him the frying pan. "Legitimate Teflon coated frying pan, no funny business, right?" I gave it a knock for good measure and he gave me the go ahead.

I started rolling it up.

"Hey, it's working," I said smiling.

I finished and handed it off to the officer who gave it a look over.

"Wow cool, how did you get involved with this?" I gave him the same rundown I did with the other officers two weeks prior.

He tried to hand it back.

"Nope, yours to keep my friend. I have more of those than I know what to do with." Besides, it makes for a cool souvenir, though I worried that they were going to start pulling me over for novelty purposes.

"Hey if you see this car, pull it over, the guy will bend something for you." I put sixty-penny nails in the car just in case. They only cost me about sixteen cents so they aren't a big cost to bend like frying pans are.

Turned out the reason he pulled me over was because I came off the highway a little fast. I didn't feel like I was going fast, but I didn't get a ticket either. It only cost me a frying pan and I'm sure it made the officer's day. It was a small price to pay.

I guess if there was a moral to the story it would be to remember the humanity of a person and put yourself in their shoes. You might be able to make their day.

Before I decided to be a personal trainer and performing strongman I had ambitions to be a police officer. If I had pulled someone over that was a strongman, I would have done the exact same thing.

And hey, that's more people who know about *strongmanism*. Maybe it will inspire them to do something awesome. Either way it inspired them to let me go without a ticket.

Oh and by the way, the best way to avoid a ticket isn't to do feats of strength. It's to drive safely in the first place.

THE CONEY ISLAND STRONGMAN WORKSHOP

Chris and I had rescheduled the workshop from midsummer to December 6th, 2014. I was determined to make sure that people were able to make this one and I made sure to send out Facebook posts pretty often tagging all of the people I thought would be interested.

I went back and forth with Chris quite a bit to the point where Diara started thinking I had a bearded girlfriend. I knew and Chris knew that the success of the Coney Island Strongman Workshop and the future of performing *strongmanism* in general would depend on how happy people were with the workshop and the level of success that they reached. If nobody was happy or successful, the workshop would die out, and *strongmanism* may remain in a small subculture.

I had posted about it on Facebook and four girls I had kept in touch with wanted to jump on board. Christina Devos, Doctor Kathy Dooley, Kristin Dankanich and Doctor Kathryn Mattson. All of them, I had met through being a personal trainer in my quest to continue learning. Each one of them knew me through the Iron Tamer David Whitley and was fascinated with *strongmanism* and what goes into it. I knew they probably were going to go to the workshop for the same reasons I started with Greg in the first place.

They wanted to learn what separates Superman from Clark Kent.

They didn't have ambitions to be active performers, but then again I didn't either but that changed when I started getting better at the feats, knew I could talk in front of a crowd and could see that I could use this to help inspire people towards better things for themselves.

Another attendee was one of my personal training students, Tom, who helps me out with social media and was in the midst of a personal transformation. He asked me if I thought it would be a good thing for him to start up.

"Well, I don't know what your path is, I know for me *strongmanism* was a life changing journey and I know that Chris is a great coach. Whether or not you want to take the step is up to you."

He took the step.

Sometime during the marketing of it, Doctor Rob Gilbert brought me in to talk and perform for his students.

Recently, I had asked Doctor Gilbert to mentor me in the ways of the motivational speaker saying to him that I thought I could better serve the world by nailing down the message and using the feats as an illustration. He saw the value in it, so he attended the workshop even though he wasn't able to stay the entire time. Doctor Gilbert had been doing motivational speaking for over thirty years and was always adding to his talks. He was a last minute registration and someone I was excited he was going to experience some of the things he has had me illustrate for his students and attendees. What he brings me in to do; he would at some level be able to do himself. At the same time, I would have both my coaches in my studio face to face.

During the marketing of the workshop, I mentioned that I was going to do a segment on how I put *strongmanism* into the free presentations I do for local businesses and non-profit groups near my studio. Murphy's Law would soon come into effect.

Two days prior to the workshop my hard-drive crashes while I was upgrading the software and I lost my presentation along with a lot of other stuff. Luckily I had saved the copy of this book into my email otherwise I would have lost about two hundred written pages.

I stayed up 'til late hours of the night creating the new presentation so I could do my segment of the workshop, including creating the new videos for the music that would play in the background while I was demonstrating the feats.

Chris had the address of my gym and I told him to give me a call when his GPS told him he was half an hour away. I needed all the sleep I could get because I knew this was going to be a long day. It was a long time in the making and it had been a long night redoing the presentation on my new hard-drive.

I closed my eyes and the morning came way too soon. Chris needed me to be there an hour earlier than the workshop started so I could unlock the doors and set everything up.

Chris was going to kick-start the workshop with a strongman show done in his style with his story. This also marked the first occasion that I would see Chris as a standalone performer and could see what he does.

Chris arrived before me, looking more energetic than me even though he was likely running on even less sleep than I was. I arrived and found him chatting with one of the neighbors who likes to hang around outside.

"Hey Chris!" I said as I shook his ridiculously strong hand. "I hope I didn't keep you waiting long."

"Nah, I just got here about five minutes ago. Just chatting with your neighbors."

I took him for a tour of my place so that we could figure out the best way to set up. Then we took a whole lot of steel bars, phone books, boxes of decks of cards, nails and bolts and some of the various things he bent out of the back of his truck and into my studio.

"Yeah… there's going to be a lot of breakthroughs today." He said giving me his determined look.

"It's going to be epic and it's all going to happen here…at Eric Moss Fitness," I said back to him. I used that catchphrase often with my regular clients as a joke.

As we were setting up, I heard a voice outside talking to one of the neighbor's dogs. I go outside and from the back; I couldn't tell if it was Christina Devos or Dr. Dooley.

"Howdy, did you have any trouble finding the place?" I said, getting her to turn around so I would know who she was.

"Hey!" Christina turned around and gave me a hug.

Christina was the one who had introduced herself awhile back as one of my "fans." She had about her a nurturing type quality that makes her feel like an older sister. Her power comes out like scattered energy. When she finds focus it comes out as unbridled enthusiasm. When you look in her eyes, there is an intensity there that I find difficult to describe. There's something there that tells you that she has wisdom from a tough journey of self-discovery.

On top of that wisdom it almost feels like she has an ability to see you for who you really are behind the identities that we all carry on our exterior. Luckily, she seemed to think I was a pretty decent guy.

Maybe I am.

She was interested in the mindset of a strongman. I was interested in her esoteric views and would later ask her to help me find my spirit animal as I continued on this journey of self-discovery. We have a kinship, which I believe comes from being journeymen.

She came baring a bloodstone gem as a gift. An item meant to help heal. I clutch it anytime I'm going through a rough period.

"Thank you, and welcome to my place," I said smiling at her. I was happy to be a part of introducing her to the wonderful world of strongmanism. I was happy to be a part of everyone's introduction actually because *strongmanism* has done so much for me and I wanted everyone to know what I know.

That we are all capable of so much more than we think we are.

One by one, they started arriving, for the most part greeting each other with hugs. Most of the people here had met and bonded through previous strength workshops affiliated with personal training. Some of them were meeting for the first time and I was introducing them to Chris.

I started to feel the effects of not having had time to get caffeinated in the morning. I made a blanket announcement that I was going to the Quick Chek in front of my studio to get coffee and offered to get some for anyone who wanted one. Dr. Kathryn Mattson offered to take the walk with me.

As we were in Quick Chek making our coffee she asked about how I ended up being a strongman and I told her about Greg and how after he passed I was left progressing slowly. It wasn't until I had Chris in my corner that I started to make fast progress again. A good coach and a good student are a powerful mix.

I didn't want to spoil it because I was going to introduce Chris at the beginning of the workshop as he kicked it off with his own strongman show. We still had about twenty minutes 'til that point.

The good doc insisted on paying for my coffee even though I was planning to pay for hers. She had traveled two hours that morning to come to my place and I figured it was the least I could do.

We walked around back and I found Tom had arrived and so had Dr. Gilbert. This was uncharted territory for Tom, even more so than most. Tom was a stranger to *strongmanism* and to strength training until just a couple months prior when we happened to be at a party for a mutual friend and I overheard him turn down a drink because some nutrition supplement had him feeling strange. Whenever I hear something like that my senses are on alert, I talk to him about what I do and he's sold on my philosophy.

Tom had worked previously with a personal trainer who had advised him to "eat peanut butter and jelly sandwiches for energy and take fat burning supplements for fat loss." That advice is ridiculous, but Tom didn't know any better. I mean after all, this is a certified personal trainer…a paid professional giving this advice. But just like any profession, some are better than others.

So when Tom started training under my direction, this was all completely new to him. In six months he went from lost to training to be a strongman, having never heard of it before just a couple months prior. I could see he was unsure how to fit in since most of the attendees who were here knew each previously and had already bonded. That would change soon though.

Dr. Gilbert was analyzing Chris' scrollptures and the "S" bends he had done with some wrenches. One of the traits of Dr. Gilbert is he is a very curious person and is always seeking out knowledge. It's what had led him to the AOBS dinner where I originally met him to learn the psychology that goes into being a professional strongman right from the top guys.

"Hey Doc," I said greeting him in the back of the room. "Welcome to my place." I had been to his classroom many times before. Now he was in mine.

Dr. Dooley had signed up with a fellow named Eric Chessen who I hadn't met previously, so I greeted him with the same joke I always say whenever I meet someone who has my first name "Hey, great name you got there." He replied with some humorous sarcastic remark drawing a laugh.

"Another sarcastic person named Eric? In the end…there can be only one," I replied quoting the Highlander movie series. ☺

After another couple of minutes of chatting people up, it was time to get this thing going. I gathered everybody to take a spot on the mat or in chairs as I gave Chris an introduction.

"Hey everybody, I appreciate you all coming out to my place. Most of you know me previously and are well aware that I am a professional old-time performing strongman but what you might not know is that I attribute old-time performing strongmanism to saving my life. It wasn't that long ago that I was going through an incredibly difficult time in my life where I wasn't even sure I wanted to go on living. There were times when I didn't even have the strength to get out of bed. It was during this time that my first mentor, New Jersey's Superman Greg Matonick, offered to teach me the ways of the old-time strongmen and the hope to be a part of something so unique and amazing but so rare that it doesn't even have a Wikipedia page, is what pulled me through. I made great progress but when my first mentor Greg was taken, I was left to try to figure the rest out on my own…until Chris. Chris is a multiple world record holding top-level strongman and not only is he one of strongest people in the world, but he might be the single best coach for old-time strongmanism here today. It's my honor to present the coach in Bending Steel, my personal strongman coach and friend, 'Hairculese' Chris Rider."

Chris came out, telling his story of how he became a strongman, overcoming the adversity that came with a back injury and the story of his very first old-time strongman feat, reenacting it as if we had traveled back in time to the day he ripped his first phonebook.

So on and so forth it went, he told his story, destroyed something, connected us to his path, destroyed something, explained where he came from, and destroyed something. When it was said and done, there was a pile of ripped phone books, a horseshoe that Dr. Gilbert had said out loud, "That's impossible," until Chris had done it, an adjustable wrench, another wrench he broke, some decks of cards that he cornered, two frying pans rolled into a burrito and there may be some things I'm leaving out simply because there were so many feats of strength and breakthroughs that day and they are getting jumbled in my head.

The first thing Chris wanted to teach was nail driving without a hammer - you have a board of wood that is braced on top of something and you hold the nail in your hand using only a washcloth for protection. Then you slam the nail down without holding back and it will go through in one blow if you slam it down hard enough…as long as you don't hold back. It's completely mind over matter because there is a lot of fear with this feat. I had seen footage where Dennis Rogers had put the nail through his hand.

The danger is very real since Dennis is no rank amateur. What happened with Dennis, as I understand it, was a last minute glitch that caused him to be without the stands he normally uses putting him into a position where he had to try to come up with something last minute. Note the feat is relatively safe when you take the proper precautions and do it right. This is not something that should be attempted by reverse engineering a YouTube video. Proper coaching is an absolute must with this and the other old-time feats of strength. It pays to learn from people who have made mistakes so you can avoid them.

The Mighty Atom had also put the nail through his hand. In his case, he was upset by something and didn't have his mind fully on the task. If you don't fully focus on what you are doing you put yourself at risk. That goes for all of you who think you can text and drive at the same time.

The reason Chris wanted this first was because it can provide a mental breakthrough that picks up momentum for the other feats of strength. It's the same reason that Tony Robbins has people do the fire walk. One breakthrough will lead to other breakthroughs down the line.

Next up was ripping cards. One of the nice things about ripping cards is the scalability of it working up to the feat. As long as your technique is solid doing a full deck is simply a matter of time and application through incremental progression. Chris walked around fixing people's technique and I did the same. Cards were getting ripped left and right leaving a terrible mess on the floor but everybody was having a great time. This was one that Dr. Gilbert wished to learn the most and even though he had to leave the workshop early to do a speaking gig, he was so motivated the next day that he ended up doing a full deck with the things he was taught.

"This is so much fun!" I overheard Dr. Dooley say.

Everybody was doing great with the cards and was having a great time as their horizons were being broadened to include old-time *strongmanism*.

There is something about forever altering something that gives great satisfaction. I was getting to see other people do this and I loved it. I hadn't really coached these things because nobody had met my prerequisite before, but Chris knew how to progress in a way that I didn't so I followed his lead.

"This is the best day of my life!" Dr. Dooley exclaimed out loud at the sheer joy that comes from the old-time feats of strength.

"Best day of your life? And it all happened here...at Eric Moss Fitness!" I replied.

Considering how joyful a person she is with many happy days and this one had started off with the worst migraine she's had in the past two years - that statement carries a lot of weight.

Next up was bending nails. Chris started them off on easier pieces and taught the biomechanics of the short bends. There is a great level of satisfaction with these because they are steel. You are literally crushing short pieces of steel to your will and it's an excellent feeling that the students of the next generation of *strongmanism* were experiencing in my gym.

Christina had her first real breakthrough with the short bends. This was her first white out experience while bending a steel bolt and I could see the change that overtook her. It was easy to see because it is very primal. In her own words when I asked her to describe the moment she described it as a place that was "fuzzy and beautiful".

I recognized this feeling because when I was asked the same question I described it as calm and quiet. It is free of the distraction of the internal dialogue that tells you "It's too hard." or "You aren't good enough." There is nothing but you and the task. Plain and simple. It is one thing to describe it to somebody; it is entirely different to experience it for yourself.

Christina knew the power of the calm mind because of her experiences with Yoga. When she showed up at the workshop, she came bearing a gift to me of a bloodstone telling me it carried healing properties. There is a stereotype that paints Yoga practitioners as weak. Christina is one Yogi who has proved this one wrong. She is petite and has the ability to see people's auras with more clarity than most. On top of that she is very strong. I knew she was strong having seen some of the things she's posted or sent to me through text messaging or Facebook. When she later shared her story with me, I realized she was sitting on something that can potentially change lives.

The addition of *strongmanism* to her repertoire could be the big difference maker, not just for her, but for a lot of people who need help finding their path. Much like the bloodstone she brought, her story and her strength will heal people.

Next were the phone books. Chris hadn't even planned to put these in initially, but when Christina sent me a video of her trying to do it, I forwarded it to Chris and we decided to put it in there. It was a good thing too, because this was probably the most popular part of the workshop.

Christina rocked the phonebook. Once she learns to focus on the old-time feats and gets them polished and show ready, nothing will stop her. Some feats come faster to certain people than to others. The phone book came fast to Christina and also to Kristin.

Kristin's strength is unassuming, standing at five feet three inches. She is visibly muscular to the point that she looks like she trains regularly, but not to the point where she looks anywhere as strong as she is. Despite that, there is something about her that reminds me of Wonder Woman. Kristin took to the phonebooks like a fish to water. Chris had brought some small phonebooks and taught the mechanics, Kristin ripped them no problem, without "popping," without breaking the binding, without any sort of trickery. Much to our surprise, she asked to have a try at a phonebook exceeding nine hundred pages.

Not just try, she succeeded, because she put what she had into it.

Once it ripped all the way through her joy expressed itself by exclaiming "Wheee!" followed by giggling and clapping as she threw the wreckage on the floor.

The other Eric also excelled in this and Christina and Dr. Mattson soon followed, each one successfully ripping thick phonebooks. Throwing them into a pile on the floor and just having a grand old time. Then it was Dr. Dooley's turn to have a go.

Awhile back I was trying to coach her in using the mindset of a strongman to try to improve her single hand overhead press. I did what I could to try and explain it, but it wasn't fully sinking in.

I watched her struggle with the phone book. Putting what she had into it, fighting her migraine, throwing it down in disgust while it taunted her and she picked it up again. That process would keep repeating and I sat there watching the gears turning. Dr. Dooley is one of the smartest and most educated people I've ever met, having traveled the world - teaching people about anatomy - but there are some lessons you simply have to learn through experience.

Watching her struggle reminded me of the times when Greg would leave me alone with the feat. It's not done till it's complete or as Slim would say 'til the machinery breaks." If the feat doesn't break before you do, you haven't truly given it your all. I saw the phone book challenge her…taunt her…dare her to continue for about a full half an hour.

It was like that until she finally got it. Once those rips started and she felt the success she kept it going, rocking the momentum that comes with signs of progress.

I whispered to the student next to me, I can't remember who but one who knows Dr. Dooley and wanted to see her succeed.

"Look at Doc; she's finally understanding what I've been talking about," Dr. Dooley never heard me say it, because she was completely lost in the moment.

When it was all said and done one half of the book, that had one thousand one hundred eighty-four pages, remained in her hand. The other half of the book was thrown on the growing pile of destroyed phone books on the floor, the defeated adversaries lay there and she stood with a gleeful and triumphant expression on her face.

Now at this point, we had been rocking it for a long time. We didn't break for lunch 'til about three o'clock and I figured on doing my segment while everybody let their food digest.

With the no cost presentations I do for local business and non-profits, where I teach people a process for achieving their health and fitness goals, it acts almost like a nod to what the Mighty Atom and other strongmen had done in the past. Instead of doing a full show, the Mighty Atom would sprinkle feats of strength along with his health talk where he would either steer them away from things that were bad for them or sell exercise equipment and homemade health products to people who happened to see his presentation. Other strongmen of old would sell their books on how they exercised after a show.

I like to think I do a modern day equivalent where I teach people, but instead of selling supplements, I let them know if they need more help they know who to go to. Since I present a clear and simple path and remain honest amidst a sea of confusion; people often take me up on training in my studio and it's a way I get new clients.

Like an old business coach of mine had said, "If you want to reach people you have to teach people." This became the framework of how I do my talks. I insert a mini-version of a full strongman show to make the presentation more exciting. This is what I wanted to teach the trainers and chiropractors in attendance to do.

I acted like they were the lost souls who oftentimes attend my presentations instead of being knowledgeable trainers and chiropractors. I went through my intros and how I believed that coaching can be the difference maker between people who are successful and those who aren't. Then came the portion of the presentation where I bent a 60 penny nail and ripped a deck of cards (both were feats covered in the workshop). I bent the nail like it was butter and I went for a deck of cards. Chris handed me a deck that was bigger and tougher than any deck I had done previously.

"No problem," I figured. I was wrong.

This deck put up one heck of a fight and it was not going with the kind of momentum that makes for a good show, which is not something which should go into a show. I was pushing and pushing and pushing and suddenly I felt something shoot down my index finger and half of my hand lost all feeling in it.

"I seem to have damaged some nerves in my hand." Luckily it wasn't too serious though I don't think my hand will ever be the same again, but it won't prevent me from doing feats in the future. For today though, the words that Slim had said "If you don't go till the machinery breaks, you haven't given it your all." Slim would have completed the feat, but I decided to stop before more machinery broke.

For redemption I grabbed my reinforcing bar and bent it on the bridge of my nose. I wanted to make the point that these presentations are important because people want what we teach…but often times they are lost and feel like they have no hope. I cited the case studies from my presentation and also Tom's story of being led in the wrong direction at the expense of his health. People need to hear what we have to say, plain and simple, and people listen when they see these feats of strength.

Even then, though I still disappointed myself - like the wrench that got the better of me at that high school senior send off and was later destroyed - I set this deck of cards aside to return to it again at a later day.
Next came the horseshoes. When Tom had originally signed up for the workshop he said that if he could get one feat down he wanted it to be the horseshoes. In Tom's spare time he enjoys going to the racetrack so he has a special affinity for them. Chris and I walked around the room instructing people how to hold them. Tom had struggled with every other feat thus far.

With this one though, there wasn't any struggle. It just went much to his surprise. It was like everything just lined up once he put his mind to it and it caved to his will.

Suddenly a thought entered his mind that would plant a seed to change a lot of things down the line for him.

"If something I want to do comes this easy...all I have to do is put my mind to it. If I can bend a horseshoe by putting my mind to it...the possibilities are endless."

Success in one area leads to success in other areas because the principles remain the same throughout. What started out as a conversation about how to get healthy had led to experiences about how to be successful at taking charge of your life. It's funny how life sometimes works like that.

Dr. Kathryn Mattson was a surprise. She went at the feats with a natural aggression that could turn her into a star. The funny thing is that you would never have ever expected it. For anyone who doesn't know her and meets her for the first time, you would never expect such aggression, ferocity and power coming from someone like her - five foot six inches with blond hair, blue eyes, a kind smile and a soft way of speaking. Behind that smile though is a level of strength that would defy belief and had us all in a state of awe as we watched her giggling out loud as she crushed a horseshoe down on her leg.

She held up a horseshoe that she ripped open and smiled a big smile. The only sign that she had even done anything was her catching her breath...and of course the mangled horseshoe that sat in her hands. She seemed to have an innate ability to enter and leave the zone at will. It was quite awesome to see. It would be terrifying if someone made unwelcome advances on her.

And it was further proof that it is all about the mindset that you take in - unloading the power that we all have inside of us.

By the time we reached long bar bending the fatigue was starting to set in and we did what we could to teach bending steel. Bending steel is the thing that I enjoy the most simply because it was what I felt I was best doing. It was the focus of what Greg taught me and it was what I put the most time into. Despite the fatigue, the students did well. The other Eric seemed naturally proficient in this area as well.

The other Eric, I was largely unfamiliar with 'til this day. He stands at the same height as me, visibly muscular without being massive, purposefully bald and wearing glasses. Eric trains a lot of people with Autism, which is something that takes patience. He's the type that will add jokes to just about any situation to keep the mood light. You can see what a person is made of when they are giving an effort and steel is as hard as you make it out to be.

After everybody was pretty smoked from the rigors of the day we bid them well wishes. Each person had walked in the door wide eyed with wonder, excited about what they were about to learn. Each person left, even more excited but this time about their new perspective, having been successful and properly introduced to the awesome world of old-time *strongmanism*.

A couple days later, I found this on Dr. Dooley's website and she granted me permission to print it in this book.

"Dooley Noted: 12/9/2014

The best day of my life started with a migraine.

I don't get them thrice weekly, like I did at the beginning of this decade. Acupuncture

and movement therapy knocked them down to once every other month or so.

But it happens. And I can't tolerate migraine medication. So, I don't take it.

I think I've been gifted with too much energy.

Sometimes my body can't focus it.

It used to manifest in anxiety. I conquered that.

It currently manifests in migraine.

So on the morning of last Saturday's Strongman Spectacular, I was debating not going.

It was my worst migraine in 2 years.
The thought was awful. I saw myself wasting my day, laying down in pain, pitying myself.

Gross.

So, my boyfriend and I headed to the seminar.

Immediately, I felt better as I saw my beautiful friends and a few new ones I would make.

A doctor of sports psychology asked me why I craved strength.

I talked about seeing my dad at around 1.5 years old, stopping a moving car that was about to hit another car.

I knew early on that we have immense potential.

Mr. Chris Rider, professional strongman, solidified that as he bent steel in front of my eyes – with his hands.

When I saw my friends start doing the same, I believed I could do it, too.

We did. I did.

We all had a skill that was easier or more challenging for us.

Eric and Kathryn rocked almost everything.

Tom rocked the horseshoe.

Kristin and Christina annihilated the phone books.

But I struggled with the 1,184- page Las Vegas phone book.

I saw my friends do it. I knew it was possible. They cheered me on.

As I grunted and sweated, carnal yelps left me. I am inexhaustible. But I felt the energy of that migraine rise to my head and threaten to derail me.

Several minutes in, I felt myself start to give up. The lies started firing out of my mind like machine gun bullets.

"It's too hard."

"My head hurts too much."

"It was easier for everyone else."

"I'm not strong enough."

But I remembered how Chinese medicine describes migraine — as energy ascending to the head.

So, I got out of my head.

I felt every ounce of my focus zone in on that phone book.

The room was empty. There was no thought but making that book yield to my hands.

Then, I felt that book cave in to me.

I have never experienced anything as powerful as that moment.

And the migraine left me.

People that don't crave strength don't know how good it feels.

I've been painfully thin and ripped. It didn't feel like this.

I've been overweight and lazy. It didn't feel like this.

This is human potential to make the impossible probable.

After that phone book, I realized I have barely tapped into my potential.

We all have this enormous power, waiting for us to break down the door.

Some of us let the mind lie to us. I almost did. I had my entire life — until Saturday.

Now, I'm wondering what else I can do in this life.

Catalyst SPORT is bringing my new strongman skills coach, Mr. Chris Rider, to New York on Sat May 23, 2015.

The registration link is coming soon.

Mark your calendar. Move your plans. Change your life.

As always, it's your call.

– Dr. Kathy Dooley

P.S. All I want for Christmas are your phone books and playing cards. Seriously."

They witnessed their own power. They discovered their own strength. They made the coaches proud. And it all happened at Eric Moss Fitness.

BENDING STEEL ON A NINETY-THREE YEAR OLD MAN'S NOSE...SERIOUSLY, THINK ABOUT HOW AWESOME THAT IS

It was around nine on the Wednesday night before the big weekend. Chris had asked me a couple weeks back if I could bend a structural steel bar measuring five eighths of an inch thick on my nose two nights in a row. The first one would be at the Association of Oldetime Barbell and Strongman Dinner. The second one would be the following day at the Strongman Spectacular with some of the top guys...and on the two-year anniversary of when my first mentor passed...being organized by my second mentor...in an eight hundred seat theater.

"I haven't done it yet, but if that's what you think we should do...I'll make it happen."

On Wednesday night though...he called me up.

"Hey Chris, what's up?"

"Do you have any other feats that are unique?"

"I've been thinking about making a steel bar look like a paper clip, but I don't have it fully down yet. If you need me to do it at the dinner I can have it ready."

"Yeah, I might need you to do that instead of the nose bend. Bring it just in case. But something big might happen in its place, and I promise…you'll like it."

What the hell? Chris didn't want me to do the nose bend? That meant that either Slim was going to do it…or the son of the Mighty Atom, Mike Greenstein would. I had no problem bowing out in the presence of legends.

"I gotcha Chris, not a problem…kind of a relief actually." Bending steel bars on your nose is rough, especially if you don't have time to recover.

Mind over matter though.

I figured it might be funny for the audience members to tell people "I saw a strongman bend a paperclip…it was *awesome*."

The next day I took a bunch of steel bars and tried to get the measurements just right. I had never seen a steel bar bent to look like a giant paperclip so I had nothing to model off of with the exception of a small box of paperclips I keep next to my printer.

I grabbed one of the small ones, examined it, and tried to imagine what a giant one would look like.

The next day, I started cutting steel to various lengths to make sure I could get it right. I only had a short period of time to get this scroll right and debut it in front of people who were in the know. I bent a bunch of steel practicing the scroll and got it as close as I thought I was going to get. "Oh boy, I hope this goes okay," I thought to myself as I packed it away.

Dave had asked me about the different weight kettlebells I had and asked me to bring them along with some Monster Energy Drinks. Dave has a couple signature lifts that he likes to do. One being a heavy bent press and another being a mutant hybrid of a Turkish getup coupled with sledgehammer levering.

For Dave, combining a Turkish getup with levering a sledgehammer represents a nod to his journey. The getup being a part of a system of training that led him to the old-time strongmen and the levering a tribute to Slim the Hammer Man, who is a huge inspiration to him as well as to so many of the strongmen out there today, including myself.

When the day of the AOBS dinner arrived, I packed the car up with the things I'd need for the entire weekend. I packed up both of the steel bars for the nose bend (in case Chris changed his mind), the kettlebells for Dave and the bars I'd need for scrolling.

I drove into Newark and awkwardly loaded up my trolley to carry the kettlebells. At this point, I had started carrying steel bars inside of a guitar case. I had gotten the idea from the movie *Desperado* with Antonio Banderas, but none of them quite fit right. Both the bar for the nose bend and the one for the paperclip stuck out the top, causing me to awkwardly duck when I was in the doorway. Currently I keep everything in a snowboarding case. It is a much better fit.

I walked into the lobby with the guitar case with the steel protruding out the top and the trolley filled with heavy kettlebells behind me and I see Slim's great Grandson in the lobby. I recognized him from Slim's birthday party and he seemed to remember me as well.

"Howdy," I greeted him.

"Hey," he said. "Are you looking for anybody?"

"Dave Whitley and Chris Rider, have you seen either of them?"

"I think Dave went up to his room, Chris hasn't gotten here yet. Did you hear about Dennis?" he asked. Dennis Rogers had recently gotten shoulder surgery done and was thought to have hung up his cape.

"Yeah I heard. It sucks, I never got to see any of his shows," I said.

"I know," he said.

As of this writing, Dennis is getting back into the game although not at the capacity he was. You can't keep the strongman down.

"Do you think you could watch my stuff for a little bit?" I asked him. It got heavy after a while. "I'd like to have a look around and see who's here."

I walked around for a short period of time just to get an idea of the layout. I didn't want Slim's great grandson to be stuck watching my stuff. His great grandfather is a legend…and he's a fan. Truth be told I think he's going to go far in the strongman world one day. He's hanging around the right people.

I walked into the restaurant to see if Dave was in there and I found

Jonathan Fernandez eating a meal at a table by himself.

"Hey dude, what are you doing sitting by yourself? Mind some company?"

"Hey, great to see you. Please have a seat."

I could see he was happy to have some company. We discussed various aspects of being a strongman, stories from the road, what feats we like to perform and that sort of thing. As we talked, every once in a while, I looked around to see if Dave was looking for me.

Dave eventually found me and greeted me with a copy of his new book, *Taming the Bent Press*. I first tried to find the page I'm on where I am demonstrating an exercise called the front lever, and then I pulled out a pen and asked him to sign it.

"Already beat ya to it brother," he said flipping to the first few pages. In the book, I saw his signature along with the lines "Thank you for always keeping it metal." For the record, I can't really help it. Metal from birth, baby.

A little bit later Chris arrived. I had been making great progress with the things Chris was teaching me. I had added some new feats to my regular show and was very pleased that my strongman training could continue under the watchful eye of someone who had been there before.

I will always be Greg's student, but I am also a student of Chris'. In truth, I am a student of every single person whose brain I picked, whether I took their advice or not.

Anyways, Chris arrived and was doing the run around. Chris was tasked not only with doing feats of strength along with emceeing the first show; he was also the talent coordinator.

Some of the talent was late. While he was waiting for them to arrive along with trying to make sure everything was running smoothly, he pulled me to the side, along with a couple other people.

"Guys, later tonight the four of you are going to bend a steel bar on Mike Greenstein's nose."

Mike Greenstein, at the time of this writing, was ninety-three years old. Somehow I knew something like this was probably going to happen.

A hush fell over the group as the gravity of it weighed down on them. "When was the last time he did this?" I asked.

"Oh about forty years ago," Chris said, laughing a nervous laugh. Ninety-three years old…hasn't done this feat or practiced it in forty years. What could possibly go wrong?

"Don't worry, Mike knows what he is doing? Just do what he says," Chris attempted to reassure us all. Still, I was concerned, particularly because this was my finale feat and I knew exactly what went into something like this. I took a breath in and said a short prayer, "Please, God let him be okay."

I sent a text to Diara.

"I'm going to bend a steel bar on the nose of a ninety-three year old man…stay tuned." I still get a kick out of the random craziness that is my life since I started my strongman journey and I love to nonchalantly keep her informed. I always get a kick out of her reactions.

"Wait…what?!?!" she responded back.

I copied and pasted the same exact text, smiling. I knew that if everything went okay, this would be history in the making…and I was going to be a part of it.

She beckoned me for more info and I reminded her that he was the one on America's Got Talent and the same one we witnessed in Coney Island pulling a Buick with his teeth.

"OMG!" was her response. "Oh my God" was right.

It was getting closer to the time for the first stage strongman performances to start. Dave was going to be on the main stage while I was still on the first stage. My show was coming up soon, but that wasn't what was making me nervous.

I was nervous for the main event, which would be bending a steel bar on the nose of a ninety-three year old man.

"Iron Tamer…did you hear what's going on?" I asked him.

"Yup, I heard. You realize that this is going down in history, right?"

"Yeah, I know," I hadn't mentioned how nervous I was about this.

We started talking about various things regarding how to put together meaningful shows and we made a pact to help each other whenever possible. He didn't have to put it into words and we wouldn't have to shake on it because Dave and I are friends and friends help each other out. Well, real friends do anyways. Strongmen use their strength to pick others up, not put them down.

"Deal," I said as I shook the hand of the man who put me on this path to begin with. The one who introduced me to Slim who would clue me to the power I had already, to Greg who would pick up a broken man and turn him into a strongman and also to Chris who would take the strongman to the next level.

It was time for the first show. I did a one-inch by three-eighths inch steel bar, a frying pan and the paper clip scroll I had figured out just a few days prior. I guess now is as good a time as any. It turned out just as good as any attempt I had done thus far and when it was finished, I noticed Slim's great grandson in the front row, the one who had said he was looking forward to seeing me perform back during Slim's birthday and I gave it to him.

I enjoy giving out the pieces of steel that I bend because I know what kind of effect it can have on people. I remembered early on when Dave gave me the three frying pans and a horseshoe. I remembered the wrench that Dennis gave to me to use as a penholder. They are souvenirs and symbolic of the strength within. It's one of the reasons why today I bend reinforcing bars on the bridge of my nose…and save it for people fighting cancer.

Later that night, I would see on Facebook that he had fallen asleep with it still clutched in his hands. That warmed my heart for sure. ☺

John McGrath had flown in for the weekend. He is a top level strongman who gets booked internationally and yet another who had provided inspiration to me. He has a physique very similar to Slim the Hammer Man's and it's quite evident that Slim's style has influenced John's. You can see it from the way he moves…and the power he puts into his feats. After the show had completed, he looked at the scroll I had given to Slim's great grandson, analyzing it.

It's probably time to give a quick story about it. I had originally gotten the idea for a paperclip because Diara had sent a video of her then five-year-old nephew bending a paperclip on his nose.

"I like it," he simply said.

"I appreciate that, John." It was approval from one of the best today.

He put it down, looked up and was face to face with Slim. I got chills. It felt like I was looking at a promotional poster for a fight movie. Two of the best, similar build, similar style...one had influenced the other. Slim with his trademark tough guy stare. John with one of his own. Then they smiled and shook hands.

Now between the first show and the second show there was a bit of a large gap where the strongmen intermix with the crowd while the larger room gets set up for dinner, the rewards and last but not least, the main event.

Diara and I went back and forth, texting about what's going to transpire this evening and how worried I was that something was going to go wrong. None of us have been taught what to do nor had we rehearsed it. This was a huge deal.

Mike pulled us off to the side to practice in a hallway. He claimed all he needed was a quick run-through. I guessed that if Chris said Mike knew what he was doing, he knew what he was doing, so I just had to have faith. He has had more years of experience than I've even been alive. More than twice as much actually.

"Alright, here's how you do it," he said in his gravelly voice. "You put your hands here; he'll put his hands here."

The person who was having his hands adjusted was nervous and that caused him to not follow directions to well.

"No dude, here," I said moving his hand...twice...oh boy.

We were instructed to wait for the cue; "Ready, Steady, Go" and we were simply going to drop straight down. We got a dry run going and none of us were coming down at the same exact rate. That was something critical to the proper completion of the feat.

"Mike, what are you putting on top of your nose?" I asked. "Not even just for a little bit of a cushion, but also to prevent the mill scale from going in your eyes."

"Oh I'll just use this napkin," he replies…a napkin…that's it? If you recall, last year at this event Sonny couldn't believe that I used nothing more than a shop rag. This was a napkin and a ninety-three year old man.

"I have rags and wraps in my car if you want me to grab them," I offered, hoping he would take it. Nope, he was set on the napkin. Okay, Mike knew what he was doing I guessed.

I got down on my knees and said a quick prayer for his safety anyways. Mike's 'kid brother' Jerry, struck up a conversation with me about how he had tried to talk him out of it. He wasn't the only one either. Mike had nothing to prove to anybody after all. I guess Mike wanted to do it for himself, because he still could.

At this point it was time for the dinner and award ceremony prior to the main event and I was at the table with Chris Schoeck, Dave Whitley, Jonathan Fernandez, his girlfriend, Katie, and two of the Mighty Atom's sons. The son on the left was the one whose nose was going to bend steel. Dave and I were talking back and forth about the events of the day and the events still to come. Jonathan Fernandez was going to be on the main stage sometime after Dave.

Dave and I were in the middle of a conversation when Chris Schoeck interrupted us to provide me with some advice.

"Hey you know what you should do?" he said. I looked up to see what bit of advice he was going to share. "You should shave your arms. It's what people will focus on."

I pretty nearly busted out laughing. This wasn't the type of advice I was expecting that was for sure. Especially since I'm not a hairy individual.

"Uhm, okay. Thanks, I'll keep that in mind," I replied. I might take strength advice or advice on feats from him. But if my arms were hairy, I'm sure Diara would have said something about it.

"I appreciate the effort, Chris, but I think I'm okay."

Dinner arrived; the lengthy speeches for the achievement awards began. While they talked, we kept quiet for the most part, but my thoughts wandered to the events to come that evening. As I sat across from the Greenstein's, I couldn't help but wonder if something were going to go wrong. I sat there hoping that it would be okay. Repeating to myself "Mike knows what he's doing. Just do what he says."

It was time for the show to start. Dave was on deck with his hammer getup that has become a unique feat for him. It was a combination of two of the paths that led him here. Before he began, he cranked up the energy to get this place lit up. After the speeches, we needed a bit of energy.

His show went like a pro. Dave has the mindset of a rock star using *strongmanism* as his medium. I'm the same way and incorporate many of the same concepts. It's not just about doing the feats, it's using the feats to entertain and inspire people.

Jonathan was up next with a very impressive array in his repertoire. Vertical tears, coins, horseshoes in his teeth. Jonathan is an impressive strongman who sets a very high bar. Luckily, this isn't a sport. The only competition we have is with our negative self-talk, and we are always the victors when we complete the feat.

Jonathan had been set to the main event, but this was a very special occasion because now the main event was the one I was both looking forward to and dreading at the same time.

Now it was time.

Mike Greenstein and the rest of us went up to the stage. We put the ends on the steel bar. Bill Solony, a strongman I met at Greg's gym, stood behind Mike just in case he fell backwards. The rest of us got into position and awaited the cue.

The napkin went up on his nose; he got into position and calmly said the words,

"Ready."

"Steady."

"Go!"

And we dropped down like we were instructed. Even though the first attempt slipped off his nose, I saw and pointed out that he had 'kinked' the bar. He could have stopped there but he wanted to keep going.

"Ready."

"Set."

"Go!"

We dropped again, this time the bar stayed in position, and so did Mike Greenstein. The bar had no choice but to bend on top of his nose as he held the course.

I stood relieved and amazed at what I had been a part of and listened to the applause and the cheering for this little old man, who had steel bent on his nose. One of the sons of the Mighty Atom and I got to be a part of it.

Slim walked up to the stage and stood eye to eye with Mike. Both men had done amazing things. Both have legacies. Slim, one legend to another simply said the words into his ear.

"You're the man."

THE STRONGMAN SPECTACULAR

Chris was planning to do a big show in the old style of doing things. It was going to be a variety show, but leaning heavy on strongman, because that was the thing he was into. He had contacted some of the different strongmen who he thought to be top of the line and when he said he wanted me to be a part of it, I was honored.

It was going to be a non-speaking role (bummer - because I like to talk). I'd be getting paid for it but that wasn't the important thing. I was lumped in with some of the top guys of today and that made me happy. I got to share the bill with the guys I looked up to because they are top of the line. Other popular "strongmen" (I put that in quotes for a reason) were denied entry to the bill because they weren't up to the standard of quality.

Yeah, the wannabes' feats sound and look impressive, but when you are known to tamper with the feats in advance to make them easier it leads to guilt by association and we didn't want to be associated with any of that. Honesty and integrity are forefront with being a legitimate strongman. We are legitimate. We are real strongman.

Chris contacted me weeks in advance to try and plan this thing out to make it a fun show to watch. The cast was a who's who of top-level strongmen and for me to be on the list, on the two-year anniversary of when Greg passed was yet another great way to pay proper tribute to him.

The other strongmen who were there included Chris Rider, John McGrath, Jonathan Fernandez, Mike Gillette, Niko Huslander and yours truly. Adam "The First Real Man" Rinn would be emceeing the event and a trick roper named Chris McDaniel would be adding a bit of variety to the show. Later on a very special guest would be on the stage and would have made it huge for Greg.

"I'll keep my schedule clear for that day, Chris." That day also happened to fall on the two year anniversary of when Greg passed away. I'd have to bring his shirt out of retirement.

"I'd like you to bend a structural steel bar on your nose again and to do the frying pans. Would you be able to pinky lift - a fifty-three pound kettlebell and write something on the board that would be legible for an eight hundred seat theater?"

Eight hundred? Whoa. The bigger the crowd, the more amped up I get. I wasn't worried; I was looking forward to it.

"I haven't done it before but I'll give it a go," I replied.

So I started training the lift to make sure I could do it. The first time I tried it, I started light at around thirty-six pounds.

Ouch! It felt like my tendons were going to rip out of my arm. And "Ouch" was what I was supposed to write in twelve to fourteen inch letters. Oh boy this one was going to be rough.

As the weeks went on, I figured out how to do it in a manner that didn't hurt and treated the lift like practice. First, I would practice lifting the weight. Then I would make it heavy enough. Then would come just getting the weight into position. Then I would pretend to write. Then I would actually write. Then I would try to do it in front of an eight hundred-seat theater. Incremental progression is key to learning any skill.

The day finally arrived. It was the day after the Association of Oldetime Barbell and Strongman Dinner where I bent the steel bar on Mike Greenstein's nose at ninety-three years of age. I woke up early in the morning to make sure I would be there on time. I made some extra coffee because this was going to be a long day and I didn't have nearly as much sleep as I would have liked. Oh well, the show must go on.

Chris wanted everyone to "match his brand." There are certain things you expected to see that helped brand an individual. My "brand" people would be expecting was a picture of me that Diara's sister had taken at the Tricks for Breadsticks Fundraiser where I was wearing the shirt Greg gave me, which I had intended to retire. This was the perfect event to bring Greg's shirt out of retirement because this was a big old-time strongman show. Something Greg would have wanted to go see, and I was going to be there, on stage.

The drive took me over two and a half hours and I arrived to the theater ahead of time. Chris and the other guys had gotten a bite to eat and weren't back at the theater yet, so I tried to take a caffeine-inhibited nap (I had enough coffee in me to wake a corpse - so not happening). Instead I burned some motivational CDs for me to listen to when it was time to go home later that night.

When I walked through the doors of the theater to get my head on straight, some of the guests had already arrived, and they were no ordinary guests. In the audience would be Slim "The Hammer Man" Farman and Mike and Jerry Greenstein. The up and comer was going to be in front of the veterans, the legends. In the performing strongman world, they don't get much more legendary than this.

I asked the Greensteins to sign my Mighty Atom book, which they were happy to do.

"Thank you, I'm honored" I told them.

"No we're honored that you're keeping this tradition alive. Honor us by doing a good job up there" Jerry said. I smiled back and thought "I will, or I'll break myself trying."

"Yes sir." I said before walking backstage where I could keep my book safe.

The guys got back and we went through the door and found our way to the back of the theater where some of the other strongmen were signing posters and the programs. One guy was chatting up a storm regaling some of his tales. I recognized him from his Facebook page and seeing some of the videos of him on YouTube and various other web-based video platforms, including one where he set a world record for most arrows broken on the throat (where the arrowhead is driving into the throat, not likely to be the most comfortable thing in the world, but feats of strength aren't derived out of the comfort zone normally). His name was Mike Gillette and he was once described, as having "a biography that would read like an action adventure novel." Having been involved in counterterrorism to being the bodyguard for top-level executives, Bill Gates and stars like Sylvester Stallone and being a performing strongman, I'd say it's probably a pretty accurate description.

He was the *bodyguard* for *Rambo*. Think about that one for a second.

One sense, I didn't get from him was a sense of ballooning his chest (people sometimes get overinflated egos, especially in the strength world and when they have the Napoleon complex). Mike, being on the smaller size like me, was quite simply confident in his abilities. It was advertised without being advertised, if that makes any sense. He was friendly, but if you tried something, he could kill you before you hit the floor.

Niko Huslander is a big strong guy who made a name for himself in the powerlifting world. He was actually a newcomer to the scene, but Chris picked him out because he was a natural entertainer who was simply competing rather than being on an actual stage. He was a good pick because he really was entertaining. He was going to be doing a one handed dead-lift of about four hundred pounds. He was a very spiritual man, like Greg had been, using his strength to lead people towards a greater good.

Jonathan Fernandez was a phenomenon, the one to destroy us all if he were to be persuaded by the dark side of the force. The man's strength was deceptive because he looks like a normal human being, but the feats he can do are absolutely astounding. I witnessed him bending coins, both in his fingers and in his teeth. That is extremely rare. He had spent time in isolation with monks prior to becoming a strongman.

John McGrath was the strongman from South Africa. His abilities at bending steel were amazing and he ripped through a wicked steel bar turning it into a scroll resembling one that Alexander Zass had made famous. I watched his every move to see how he did it because this was a real professional entertainer at bending steel. And his abilities with the hammers are surpassed only by Slim the Hammer Man himself.

Chris McDaniel was a world record holding trick roper. It seemed odd to have him in the show, but it made for a nice variety. He was sometimes nicknamed "the show stealer" for his abilities to entertain and today would likely be no different. His ropes going just a couple feet over the audience's heads transfers very well a live stage.

Of course I don't need to give Chris an introduction. Chris was both performing, coordinating the event and living on the edge of chaos, which just happens to be Chris' comfort zone. He loves being in the thick of it.

Part of the show would involve Chris making a terrible mess by ripping through phonebooks like they were pieces of wet tissue paper and throwing the torn pages all about much to the dismay of the little old janitor on stage...

The janitor, who would rip off his disguise and reveal that he was Mike Greenstein, the son of the Mighty Atom and the oldest performing strongman. This would be awesome to Greg, to see me on stage with the Mighty Atom's son doing what he taught me to do.

Afterwards the plan was to have me go out to bend the steel on my nose to pay tribute to the Mighty Atom, who had inspired so many of us that day. I said to Adam Rinn (the emcee) as he was putting down the finishing touches on the script, making it adaptable in case there were any last minute changes.

"Can we also mention that I'm doing it to tribute Greg Matonick, too? It's been two years to the day and it would mean a lot to me," I said.

"Has it really been two years?" Adam, the first real man, said as he looked up in surprise.

"Yeah," I replied nodding.

"Wow," he sat back in his seat reminiscing. "You know my deepest regret is that I never went down to his place to learn from him. Of course, I'll mention him. Thank you for letting me know."

"I appreciate it," I said relieved. I knew this needed to be a pretty tightly run ship, but I would have been upset if he wasn't mentioned. Greg's name was still alive in the strongman world and will remain so as long as I have something to say about it.

All of us continued to chat as we continued to sign the posters and programs. Last minute prep for the show then we waited.

A bunch of us backstage had huddled around the TV monitor that had a view of the stage so we could watch the show. Some of us would pace back and forth getting ourselves ready. I did a mixture of the two.

I was set to be out twice. The first time following Niko where I would roll up the three frying pans. The second time after the intermission, after Mike Greenstein gets out of his disguise and talks about his father. I was going to tribute the Mighty Atom and Greg Matonick by bending a steel bar on my nose. When asked what I had to say about that I would pick up the fifty-three pound weight with my pinky and write "ouch" on the board in twelve to fourteen inch letters.

I wouldn't need long to get myself ready for the frying pans. That one didn't really need any mind over matter mind prep work. I would only need to shake out some of the nerves prior to being in the forefront of an eight-hundred seat theater.

I watched the others do their thing, and made sure I had everything ready. In this case the only thing I needed was all three of the frying pans.

Niko was out there screaming, "I want more weight!" having a funny segment with Adam, the emcee, where Adam is saying there is no more weight, the gyms are fresh out of barbell plates.

Then Niko gave a short speech about his story of overcoming adversity. I heard my name called and I walked out, cool and confident, smiling and waving to the audience, with all three frying pans in my hand. I was holding one in my hand and tossing the other two onto the stage intentionally making a loud noise. They needed to hear the loud noise because Niko was loud and I didn't want to have a big contrast. Besides hearing the clanging of the frying pans let them know that they aren't made of rubber.

The lights were focused on the stage of the theater leaving the audience in the dark where I couldn't see them. Oh well, I knew they were there so I held the first frying pan up and gave it a knock so they knew it was real. Then I rolled it up and broke off the handle. Then I took the second frying pan and rolled it around the first one and broke off the handle. Then I rolled the last one around the first two and bowed in gratitude to the audience and strolled off the stage. This particular crowd was very responsive and they cheered nice and loud. First bit done and rocked. That was the lesser of two evils though.

I walked backstage bumping fists and shaking hands with the other performers as they congratulated me on a job well done.

"How'd I look?" I asked the guys huddled around the monitor.

"Looked great from here," one of them said.

"Okay, good," I said relieved.

Some of the other acts went on prior to the intermission. The music stopped, the audience chatted amongst themselves at what they had just seen, stood up, stretched and got blood back in their legs. I'm sure some of them used this opportunity to use the rest room.

I was back stage still, doing last minute stuff I needed to do but there really wasn't much so I just hung out awaiting the time when it would be my turn again.

Intermission was over and I was watching Chris through the monitor ripping phonebooks like tissue paper. Chris holds world records in phonebook tearing and it's his pet feat. He was out there doing what he loves; making a mess throwing everything around and Mike Greenstein was out there disguised as a janitor acting mad. It was pretty entertaining.

Then Adam "The First Real Man" announced we had a special guest while "the janitor" was trying to clean up the mess.

"You may have seen him on America's Got Talent. The son of the Mighty Atom, Mike Greenstein."

Mike pulled off his fake mustache and started talking about his dad and the history of the strongmen. At ninety-three years of age he was the one who had seen it all and I was honored that I was going to be on the same stage, yet again, with the legend.

It was now my turn to come out. I brought the five-eighths inch thick polished structural steel bar and the fifty-three pound weight with me. I didn't see a board or pad of paper to write on.

Maybe they'd bring it out afterwards.

"To pay tribute to the Mighty Atom, Eric is going to bend this structural steel bar measuring five-eighths inch thick on the bridge of his nose. He was taught this feat by Greg Matonick who passed away two years ago today and this is done to honor him as well."

"Thank you, Adam."

I held the bar up trying to make the lights reflect off it, some advice that Slim gave me prior to the show.

Adam beckoned for the countdown to begin.

"Ten." Here we go again.

"Nine."

"Eight."

"Seven."

"Six."

"Five." Breathe out.

"Four." Breathe in.

"Three." Breathe out.

"Two." Breathe in.

"One." Boom! I pulled the steel down hard on my nose and it gave way just like every other time I had done it. Thank you, Greg, for teaching me this and thank you, Adam, for helping me keep his name alive. Thunder from the audience.

"Eric is there anything you'd like to say about that?" That was my cue to do the pinky lift and write "ouch."

I took a quick look around and didn't see anything to write on. Well maybe they'd bring it out once the weight is in position. I pulled out my pen, uncapped it and lifted the weight up with my pinky and held it there for about ten seconds.

No pad yet, and the audience was waiting for me to do something so I put the weight overhead with one hand and absorbed the applause.

When it was time, I put it down on the ground. Okay, no writing I guess but I still did something.

"And he's going to write it, on this piece of paper," Adam said with a grin holding up a flimsy piece of paper that was about six inches by eight inches.

Oh boy, I had a hard time writing legibly without a weight, now I had to do this twice, on that little piece of paper.

"Suck it up and do what you can," I told myself. "You're a strongman and being a strongman means making it happen."

I picked the weight up with my pinky again and did my best to make it halfway legible. My hands were shaking making it really difficult to write on this piece of paper.

Adam being quick on his feet said, "And he's written it in ancient Sanskrit...translated I think it says 'ouch'." Excellent recovery!

Afterwards they focused the up-close camera on the coins that Jonathan Fernandez was going to bend. Bending coins in the teeth is an incredible feat that Greg was known for. On a big stage special things need to be done so that people can see what's happening. Luckily they planned this out far in advance and had a projector and screen. I watched from the backstage on the monitor happy as anything. Even though it wasn't announced, Jonathan was doing it also to honor Greg, who inspired him to do the feat in the first place. When he got back, I shook his hand.

"Greg would have been proud," I told him

"Thank you. Eric you've been very supportive, I want you to have this," he said as he handed me the coin.

I held it in awe and a bit of disbelief. Then I handed it back to him saying that I thought he should send it to Greg's family. He handed it back yet again promising that they would get one, too. Jonathan, if you are reading this I was honored that you gave it to me. I'm sure Greg's family will feel the same.

Jonathan's girlfriend Katie came into the back before it was time to walk out as a group on stage and said that it was a great show. More fun than shows she had previously seen (this had been planned out far in advance). She then told me that she was behind some girls who were whispering things about how "cute" I was.

I laughed and held up my fist like the success kid meme and said, "Doing it right, I can't wait to tell Diara how in demand I am." I was laughing as I said this but there are worse things than being known as a heartthrob amongst the supermen. Honestly though, I think it's just because I dress halfway decent and I look approachable. At least I hope I do.

And yes, I am approachable. I enjoy talking with people after the show, before the show etc. Just remember, when I'm doing the show, I'm in the zone.

Time came for the final curtain call; we all walked out onto the stage one at a time. The applause was thunderous and the spotlight blinding. Here I was, sharing the stage with the top guys today in front of some of the legends that inspired us. You remember how I wanted to be one of the top guys at something? Well there I was. And I was loving it.

After the show, after signing autographs, I saw Slim eyeing me in the parking lot.

"Hey Slim. How'd I do?" I asked the legend.

"You did well," The legend replied. "If you want to know how you did, listen to the crowd. They'll let you know if they like it or not."

I stood in front of the legend who was still incredibly strong as he stood over me. He took a moment to start regaling me with some of his tales.

"The biggest and loudest crowd I ever performed for was in front of about twenty thousand people at Madison Square Garden. The energy was deafening."

My imagination wandered to images of Slim on stage with the Atom, in front of twenty thousand people. I imagined what it must have felt like, what it would be like if it was me on that stage. I recalled the words Greg had said to me.

"Set your mind on what you want to do."

Nothing is impossible.

AFTERWORD

As I sit back and read my own book, having reflected on the journey I've been on, it makes me ponder what the future holds.

Even between the time I had completed the writing of this book (while I was in the process of editing) I've had even more stories happen that I guess will just have to wait for another book.

Ok, I'll tell a quick one.

One day, when I returned to Doctor Gilbert's classroom to perform, I brought a book he had previously given me and I asked him to sign it. Doc wrote a note for me and one line struck me as the perfect way I should end this book.

"Eric, you are the *future* of the old-time strongmen."

Yes, because the journey is not over. My journey, the strongman's journey, has just begun.

My first mentor, "New Jersey's Superman" the late Greg Matonick in his gym. Greg was a life changer and a great man.
(Photo credit Kira Matonick)

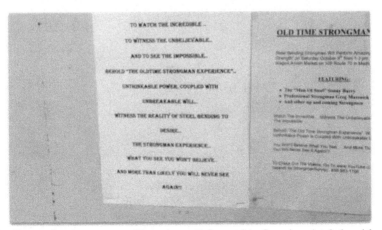

The line "The Strongman Experience" from this flyer inspired the title of this book.
(photo credit Kira Matonick)

Horseshoes, some new and some ripped open by Greg, on the wall of Atlas Railings.
(Photo credit Kira Matonick)

The chain that crossed Greg's gym was made of hand bent nails, holding
hand bent spikes and hand bent wrenches.
(From the author's collection)

First steel bar I bent on my nose, in Greg's gym, the day he said I'm
officially a strongman
(photo taken by Greg, from the author's collection)

Greg bending a reinforcing bar on his nose.
(Photo credit Kira Matonick)

A quarter bent in the teeth of Jonathan Fernandez at the Strongman
Spectacular. Greg inspired him to do this feat.
(author's collection)

Pictures of Greg and feats of strength decorating Slim's Dungeon
(author's collection)

A promotional poster from when Greg was an active strongman
(photo credit Kira Matonick)

Both of my strongman mentors. Greg and Chris.
(photo credit Kira Matonick)

Bending a steel bar on my nose for my birthday to raise money for St. Jude's, so sick kids can have more birthdays.
(picture taken by Mark Mogavero)

Driving my dream car after a performance at a car show. The generosity of some people is unbelievable.
(author's collection)

This was the car I totaled. I bent a wrench for the cops who picked me up an hour later.
(author's collection)

Giving my autograph to Ashley Massaro
(author's collection)

The first class from the Coney Island Strongman Workshop.
Top left going right. Myself, Eric Chessen, Chris Rider, Tom Daly
Bottom going right. Christina Devos, Kathy Dooley, Kathryn Mattson,
Kristin Dankanich.
(credit Tom Daly)

Myself and Bud Jeffries after a school assembly
(from the author's collection)

Bending 60 penny nails with Chris Rider
(photo credit Chris Rider)

This picture was inspired by one I saw of Slim performing with the Mighty Atom looking on from the heavens. I thought it would be a great way to tribute my mentor Greg.
(author's collection)

Myself with Slim the Hammer Man Farman in Coney Island. I bent that steel bar with my nose for him to put in the dungeon.
(author's collection)

Christina Devos, Kathy Dooley, Kristin Dankanich and Kathryn Mattson
grinning ear to ear at the joy of destroying phonebooks.
(photo credit Eric Chessen)

A selfie with Diara
(author's private collection)

Strongman selfie with "Hairculese" Chris Rider.
(Author's collection)

The lineup of some of the Olde-Time Coney Island Strongman
Spectacular. From the left going right is Jonathan Fernandez, John
McGrath, Mike Gillette, Chris McDaniel (a world record holding trick
roper), myself, Niko Huslander, Chris Rider and Adam "The first real man"
Rinn. It was an honor to share the stage with some of today's top
strongmen in front of some of the legends.
(Photo credit Katie Angell)

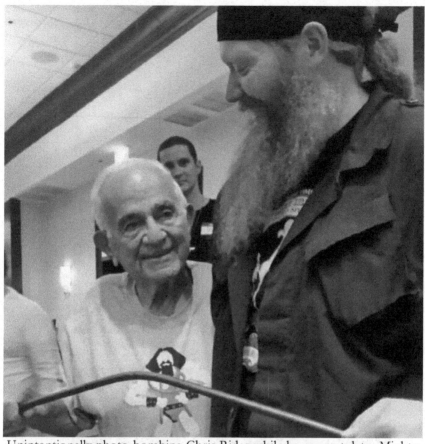
Unintentionally photo-bombing Chris Rider while he congratulates Mighty
Atom Jr. (Mike Greenstein) after we bent a steel bar on his nose at 93 years
old.
(photo from Chris Rider's collection)

Pulling 5/8ths inch round structural steel down on my nose at AOBS while Chris Rider acts as emcee. I did this to honor Greg with his favorite feat. (author's collection)

The first hand bent steel "scrollpture" I ever did.
(photo taken by Greg, taken from the author's collection)

Greg's gym was no regular gym.
(photo credit Kira Matonick)

Dr. Dooley showing the steel bar her newly discovered power at the Coney Island Strongman Workshop in my studio. The "ouch" written on the paper on the wall was from my practice run for the pinky lift with weighted writing for the Strongman Spectacular.
(photo from DrDooleyNoted.com and used with permission)

"Iron Tamer" Dave Whitley and myself keeping it metal.
(photo from author's collection)

That's all folks. My final bow at the Tricks for Breadsticks fundraiser.
(photo by Lynda Renee Photography)

THANK YOU

Yes I wrote this book on my own without using a ghostwriter or anything like that and can take complete credit for the writing end…but I wasn't alone in this. I have so many people to thank who made this dream become a reality.

"Hairculese" Chris Rider, Todd Jones, Diara "beautiful girl" Kwartler, Levi Rivas, Kira Matonick, Kip Scott, James Waselkow, William Sproat, Melody Schoenfeld, Kathryn Mattson, Robert Lebron, Jesse Vince-Cruz, Robert Nejedly, Rene Ricafranca, Kimberly Lynn, Sarah Mercado, Joseph Miranda, Esther McCrea, Rich Monahan, Jonathan Fernandez, Will Friedrich, Rob Newman, Costin Ignat, Michelle Bonelli, Amy "The Honeybadger", Linda Wagner, Tom Daly, Pam Fullerton, Dan Weinheimer, Ian Borukhovich, Diane Miranda, Kim Squero and Christina Devos

Mom and Dad for everything you guys have done. Greg Matonick for his teachings, Chris Rider also for his teachings, Dr. Rob Gilbert for mentoring my message delivery. Jaime Vendera, Stephanie Clark and Geo Derice for advice and helping put this together. Kira Matonick for photo contributions and for support. Jesse Vince-Cruz for helping my computer get up and running each time I broke it…which was A LOT. Kristin Dankanich with Project X Creative and Renee Lynn Photography for the book cover. Diara Kwartler for her patience and understanding with me throughout all of this.

And last but not least a big thank you to you the reader for reading my story. I'm so thankful you sat down and spent time reading and I sincerely hope you enjoyed learning about my experiences and what I'm so passionate about.

ABOUT THE AUTHOR

Eric Moss is a fitness professional, author, professional performing strongman, motivational speaker, and philanthropist. He spends his time coaching his personal training clients at Eric Moss Fitness, getting attacked by his cat "The Batman", catching people in "that's what she said" jokes, frustrating his fiance, rocking out to heavy metal music and watching superhero movies. He resides in Hopatcong New Jersey.

You can learn more about him on his websites www.StrongmanEricMoss.com, www.EricMossFitness.com or catch him on facebook.com/StrongmanEricMoss or his instagram @ericjmoss.com